Don't Make Love to Me…Fuck Me!

A Novel by

Nicole Scott

Don't Make Love To Me...F*ck Me!!!
All Rights Reserved
Copyright © 2014 by Nicole M. Scott
AMB/KENERLY PRESENTS

ISBN 10: 06-923-4311-3
ISBN 13: 978-0602-3431-11

Ohio

Printed in the United States of America

"Sex is an emotion in motion" – Mae West

Geena

Introduction

The warm water spewed from the shower head massaged the crest of my lower back as I leaned forward with my arms out before me, hands against the light blue tiled wall underneath the shower head with my fingers spread open. My head tilted down as I bit down on my bottom lip gently sucking it as my eyes slowly closed. I felt her finger gently and gracefully slide up my back following the crease that hid my spine; a tickling yet electrifying type of feeling. As her hand went up, she rubbed her fingers through my thick, naturally curly bronze colored medium length hair massaging my scalp. I leaned my head back towards her sighing in response. With her other hand, she cuffed my left breast running her thumb firmly across my erect nipple. I released a soft moan as she brought her other hand around and cuffed my other breast licking my neck, from my shoulder to my ear, with the tip of her tongue then gently sucked on my neck while caressing my breasts. I tilted my head to the left as her lips massaged up and down then across the back of my neck. I squirmed as I placed my hands on top of hers as she continuously strummed my nipples with her thumbs.

The feeling sent erotic vibrations throughout my body as my jewel began to pulsate. I was ready. I was ready for this as I turned towards her running my fingers through her long jet black hair and gently, slowly, and passionately kissing her lips. As we kissed, I massaged the back of her neck near her hairline with my fingertips. This excited her as our slow kiss became a fast, deep, lustful kiss. She gripped my back with her fingernails, gently scratching across. I rubbed my hands up the back of her head and gently tugged her hair. She tilted her head back gripping me tighter. I gently bit the outer edge of her ear then sucked on it. I moved down gently biting and sucking her neck. She squirmed gripping me tighter. When I got to the crest of her neck where the neck meets the shoulder, I took a big bite as I sucked her neck. She said, "Shit!" as her knees damn near faltered.

I moved my way down to her breasts. I copied her and thumbed the right nipple. I stroked the left nipple with my index finger slowly flicking up and down as I sucked on her right nipple. She pulled my hair as she began to breathe hard. I continued this switching sides for a spell as the warm water from the shower head massaged my back and her wet, thick brown body sparkled like a gemstone.

As I sucked on her breast, I rubbed my hands down the side of her trunk slowly following the natural curve of her body. I licked up her chest, sucking the water that dripped from her body licking and sucking back up to her neck. As my lips massaged her neck again, I rubbed my index finger up and down the split between her vaginal lips. She was so erect. She was so wet. As I kissed her neck and rubbed her clit, she breathed harder and harder releasing a few moans into my ear as she hugged my body tight and bit down on my shoulder.

I kissed her ear. She tilted her head up staring at me. Those eyes…those low slanted hazel eyes with those long-curly eyelashes; that erotic expression on her face like she wanted to explode – I knew she was throbbing. I kissed her lips again as she grabbed onto my shoulders gripping them and moving her hands about. I rubbed her clit in a circular motion applying more and more pressure. She loudly said, "Got Damn…Shit!"…I couldn't take it anymore. I had to have her.

I picked her up as she held one hand onto the shower bar and the other against the wall. I wrapped my arms around her thick thighs gripping onto to her behind. I licked up one lip then down the other. I licked up the middle then in a circular motion onto the clit. I began tongue kissing her clit using my tongue and lips; sucking, blowing, licking, sucking, massaging the clit like a professional. She shouted, "Uh…Uhhh…Shit…Uh."

While I was doing what I do, I felt a chilly draft. My pretty ass husband opened the shower curtain standing, watching for a spell totally naked as his perfectly sculpted chest and abs flexed; he stood erect. He climbed into the shower behind me firmly rubbing from my ass up to my shoulder. He gripped the sides of my hips as he injected his magnum gold pack sized, eight inch penis inside of me. He thrust slowly going in an out as I continued to suck on her clit. It felt so good that it was distracting me from what I was currently doing. With every stroke, he's hitting my g-spot with just the right amount of force at the precise angle. Damn I wanted to scream as he went faster and faster. "Got Damn!...Shiiiiitttt!" I shouted as I tried to keep my pace with her. Trying to hold her up while her legs trembled and thighs locked around my head as he gripped my thighs beating it up like a man that's been in prison for ten years; my knees were getting weak as she and I both released screams and moans of pleasure. Her screams heightened my arousal making me cum in record time.

I awakened with sweat beaded on my face and my vagina pulsating; body temperature on hell. My husband lying beside me snoring stomach down with his head buried into the pillow. My goodness, it was just a dream; should have known better to even consider something that electrifying being real. I stared at my husband's golden, athletic built body. His biceps perfect, and I loved the definition of his back, but I was bored out of my mind with the predictable sex…I wanted to try something new. I was sick of the gentle, passionate love-making. Instead of making love, I wanted to fuck…and be fucked…good and hard…

A Taste of the Dark Side

I stood in the kitchen in front of the sink washing the dishes. Every dish in this house was messed up, as though, I threw a dinner party. The table was full of plates, food, and dinner napkins. The stove was covered with pots, frying pans, and baking pans. There were crumbs and food droppings on the floor. There was a red stain on the tan area rug underneath the kitchen nook from someone spilling juice. Every day was the same old thing; I cleaned and cooked.

I examined my surroundings. I had half of this kitchen clean so far. I only had to wash the pots and pans, sweep and mop the floor, and clean off the table. In the meantime, I needed a break because my back was killing me. I allowed the remainder of the dishes to soak unaccompanied, as I took a seat at the Oakwood nook that rested in the corner of my kitchen adjacent to the stove. From my left apron pocket, I pulled out a cigarette, lit it, and indulged in the relaxing feeling the nicotine gave my soul each time I inhaled.

I stretched out my arms, as if, I was about to yawn then slouched in my seat. The kids were upstairs playing, and once again, my husband was having a late night at the office. This was the third time this week he had missed dinner. I worked hard to make his favorite meal, pot roast, homemade garlic bread, loaded baked potatoes, homemade macaroni and cheese, and fresh picked greens from my garden. It's 9:37 p.m. Where was he?

"Geena! Geena!" Saiaire screamed. I talked him up. I put the cigarette out in a hurry. I jumped up and opened the window to allow the smoke to escape. I began washing the rest of the dishes. Saiaire walked into the kitchen. "Did you hear me call you? Damn! What happened in here?" he asked.

"The kids and their friends," I responded.

"You're stressing?" Saiaire questioned as he walked behind me hugging me from behind.

"No, I'm not," I lied as I placed the cup I just washed in the dish rack.

"Yeah you are. I smell smoke. You only smoke when you're stressed. Why don't you take a hot bath? I'll finish cleaning this up."

"Okay," I said as I grabbed some paper towels and dried my hands.

"Hey! Where's my kiss?" Saiaire stated.

I gave him a peck on the lips then said, "I put your plate in the oven."

"Thanks. I'm sorry for missing dinner. I tried to get out of there as soon as I could," he explained while getting his plate out of the oven.

"It's okay. I know you have a very important account," I said while taking my apron off and laying it on the table.

"What are you stressing about?" Saiaire questioned as he put his plate into the microwave.

"We'll talk after my bath…okay?" I responded as I exited the kitchen.

***

While running my bath water, I was deep in thought. I love my husband. He was certainly a gift from God; I promise he was. My kids were my greatest blessings. However, I was bored out of my fucking mind. How did I let my marriage get like this? In the beginning, it was nothing like this. Saiaire and I had so much fun, and the sex? The sex was to die for. Now, the sex was routine; nothing new or exciting, simply the same tired two positions, doggy style, and missionary. To add, we didn't go anywhere unless we were taking the kids someplace they wanted to go. I had a bachelor's degree in Business Management, yet I was a housewife. If I weren't running errands, I'd sit at home all day. These walls were becoming my prison. It seemed that every person in the world had something to do except for me. This housewife shit wasn't cut out for me. I had to let Saiaire know that I wanted to start my own business.

***

As I soaked in the tub, I was irritated by my surroundings. I wanted at least one day of peace, if only I had one wish. All I heard were kids screaming, bumbling, wrestling, and my husband blasting his music. I couldn't stand the type of music he listened to. He had to be the only Mexican in the world that listened to heavy metal. I had a severe headache. This extracurricular shit wasn't helping. I didn't know how much more I could take before I snapped.

Saiaire walked into the bathroom, "Hey beautiful. Do you mind if I take the boys to mom's for the night?"

"Your mother's? Wow! It's been about a year since they spent the night over there. What's the occasion?" I asked.

"My brother's in town and he brought the boys," he explained.

"Okay, but just for one night. Bring them back early so we can go to the game."

"Your wish is my command Love. Be back soon," he said then exited the bathroom.

I needed to loosen up. I was so overprotective of my sons. I have a total of five with my oldest being twelve and my youngest being four. I couldn't help being overprotective. My husband and my boys were all I had. I grew up in foster home after foster home. I never knew my family. They got rid of me at birth. Since I wasn't lucky enough to get adopted, I had strong abandonment issues. Though I complained about the noise other people made, I hated being alone. Lately I felt alone even in a room full of people. I hated feeling like that.

I knew I shouldn't trip because my boys were with family. However, that side of the family didn't always accept them. In their eyes, Saiaire was supposed to marry another Hispanic not a bi-racial woman. I am Indian (from India not Native American Indian) and Korean. It's clear that I'm definitely the wrong ethnicity for them. When my oldest son was born, Saiaire's mother wouldn't look at him. She didn't want anything to do with him because he resembles a dark-skinned Korean. He didn't look Hispanic at all. When the twins were born, she totally clowned me. They look 100% Indian, very dark complexion and all. She told Saiaire that she didn't believe they were his sons. It wasn't until my second to my youngest son was born before Saiaire's mother began interacting with her grandsons. It's only because he look 100% Mexican. She knew that I wouldn't allow her to come to get him without taking his brothers too. In order to see him, she had to take them all. Knowing that, I was weary about letting her keep my boys. Saiaire and I had a rainbow family, and we're proud of it.

***

I'm out of the tub. I stayed in there until the water got cold. I needed that soak, that quiet time. I felt so much better now. My headache was actually going away. Who'd thought silence was medicinal?

I walked to my extremely large bedroom wearing nothing more than a towel. I hadn't been able to walk around like this in so long I felt like a woman who was recently released from prison. I felt free because every other day I felt like a Hebrew slave.

I allowed my towel to slip to the carpet. "Look at that beautiful brown skin", Saiaire said while staring at me like it's his first time seeing me naked.

"That was fast", I said while grabbing the lotion out of the linen cabinet.

Saiaire walked towards me grabbing the lotion out of my hand. "Turn around," He commanded.

I turned with my back towards him, and he rubbed lotion on my back and shoulders.

"Since the boys are gone, why don't we get busy?" Saiaire asked.

"Get busy? You mean fuck?" I blurted.

"Yeah. It's been a while."

I turned facing Saiaire then stared my fine ass husband in his eyes. I gave him a soft peck on the lips as I grab the bottle of lotion out of his hand. I replied, "What happened to us?"

"What are you talking about?" Saiaire asked with a blank expression on his face.

As I placed the lotion back into the linen cabinet, "I remember, before we got married, you'd never ask for sex. You would grab me, rip my clothes off, throw me against the wall, and fuck the shit out of me. Now, you're asking if we can get busy? I don't want to hear let's get busy Saiaire. I want you to say, 'Let me fuck the shit out of you.'"

"Okay, well let me fuck the shit out you."

"You didn't say it right! I don't know how to say this, but I'm bored," I confessed as I opened my drawer to look for some underwear.

"Bored with what?"

"Everything, especially the sex."

"You trip'n. I give good dick damn it! I've been putting you to sleep for years," Saiaire defended while sitting on the edge of the bed.

"I didn't say it was terrible because it's not. I'm saying it's boring. I want to try something different," I explained as I put on my red lace panties and matching bra.

"Like what?"

"I don't know yet. On top of that, this housewife thing isn't for me. I didn't bust my ass in school to sit at home. I want to start my own business."

"We'll talk about that later. Come on over here and let me taste you," Saiaire replied.

"I'm serious and all you can think about is sex?"

"It's hard not to. You're standing in my face half ass naked looking finer than the day I first met you. My little homey can't contain himself."

I walked to the bed and lain across it on my stomach with my head facing the headboard. Saiaire was at the foot of the bed. He leaned over pulling my leg. I kicked my leg at him to make him stop. He climbed onto the bed, and lain on top of me. He placed his head on my shoulder, "I love you. What can we do to make things better?"

"I want to start a business, and I want to spice up our sex life."

"Okay. Take $10,000 out of the account and do what you have to do to make that business happen. As far as the sex life, we do everything, oral, anal, penetration. I'm lost. You find some freaky ideas that we never tried, and I'll do it. I'm down for whatever."

"Anything?"

"Anything and I'll do it," He replied

"No boundaries?"

"None. We can get handcuffs, whips, whatever you want. In the meantime, let's enjoy each other."

"You promise anything I want with no boundaries?"

"You have my word."

Saiaire gently kissed across my shoulders as he rubbed his hands up and down the sides of my back. I squirmed a little as it tickled a bit. Saiaire grabbed me turning me onto my back. He leaned up and unbuttoned his shirt. He tossed it across the room. The definition of his muscles showed through his white tank top. I leaned up and grabbed a hold of his tank top. I gently and smoothly glided it off his body while staring into his eyes. I loved my husband's eyes. They were shaped like an almond with the long curly eyelashes. To add, they were a deep chocolate-brown matching his hair color. I couldn't help but kiss him passionately biting and sucking on his bottom lip.

He laid me down on the bed. I ran my fingers through his ponytail as I glided the ponytail holder off. Saiaire pressed himself against me thrusting and grinding reminding me of high school; we used to fuck with our clothes on.

I removed his tank top tossing it across the room. I turned him over staring intently into his eyes. He smirked revealing those dimples that melted my soul. I rubbed my hand across his chiseled chest rubbing my hands down towards his belt. I unbuckled his belt and unzipped his pants. His manhood practically popped out. I pulled his pants off tossing them onto the floor then wrapped my hand around his pole. I gently wrapped my lips around the head sucking it while rubbing up and down his pole. Normally, I would go to town until he came, but I was sick of the routine. I crawled up on him kissing his lips. Saiaire flipped me over as I felt a little disappointed because I wanted to dominate instead of always being dominated.

I had a fine, sweet husband who loved me dearly. However, I already knew what was going to happen. He was going to lick and kiss me from head to toe. Then he was going to perform oral. After that he was going to fuck me missionary style. If I was lucky, he might hit it from the back. People say it's good to know your man like the back of your hand, but this was ridiculous. Nobody's husband should be this predictable, ever!

***

It was late afternoon. My husband, boys, and I were at a minor league baseball game. The crowd, the excitement, was making my head throb. I guess it throbbed because I really didn't want to be here. I didn't like baseball at all. However, my boys and my husband couldn't survive without seeing or playing a game. Saiaire went to college tuition free from his baseball scholarship. He would have gone pro if he hadn't torn his ACL. Because of him, all of our boys played baseball. I'd rather they play soccer, but who was I to make decisions? I was so sick of this submission shit. I had a mind and opinions too; the good wife? I desired to be naughty.

I headed to the concession stand. I was hungry, and I need to escape the noise. The cheers, boos, and screams, were echoing in my ears. To add, Saiaire had been drinking. I couldn't stand when he drank. He played entirely too much, and it was so annoying. He also got horny as hell, and frankly, I was tired of fucking him.

As I headed to the concession stand, I saw Chandra. I went to high school with her. She and I had an interesting past. My goodness she lost so much weight. In high school she was 5'8" and weighed around 185lbs. She was always gorgeous as hell. Now she look like she's around 160lbs. She had the perfect hourglass figure and the straightest, whitest teeth I ever saw in person. She looked really good. I'm sort of jealous. She looked better than me now, and I was voted most attractive out of senior class.

I walked towards her, "Hey stranger."

Chandra smiled, squealed, and gave me a big, tight "I miss you" hug, "Geena! How have you been?"

"I've been good and you?"

"I'm happy. I finally got rid of Chase, and my life has been so much better," Chandra said with the largest smile on her face.

"I'm happy to hear that. You look good."

"I feel good. Are you still with Saiaire?" She asked.

"Yep! We're married with 5 beautiful boys," I replied.

Chandra stared me eye to eye for a few seconds then said, "You haven't changed a bit. You are still most attractive."

I blushed, "Nah! That title belongs to you now."

Chandra smiled lighting up the entire stadium as she pulled out her cell phone and said, "Girl what is your number? We definitely have to hook up sometime. I have to meet your kids."

"555-8273. You have any children?"

While putting my number into her cell phone, she said, "No. I will definitely call you. I have to get back before Devin gets mad. It is so nice to see you."

"You too."

Chandra gave me another hug then she walked away.

I returned to the game with a basketful of food, snacks, and drinks. My husband and children were extremely grateful. I, on the other hand, was distracted from the excitement.

Tomorrow Saiaire returned to work, and the boys returned to school. I returned to a lonely day of cleaning, cooking, washing and folding clothes. My life…what life?

Saiaire allowed me to take out $10,000 to start my business venture. Through the bitching about wanting to start my own business, I never thought about what type of business I wanted to start. The only thing I was really good at was cooking and cleaning; doubt if I remember anything from my degree program because I never used any of the knowledge. I didn't want to start a cleaning service because I actually hated having to clean up every day. I didn't want to start a daycare center. Shit, I was thrilled to get rid of my own kids for the time they were in school. Why would I want to allow more children to enter into my home? That'll be more food to cook and more items to clean. I guessed I could start a catering company. I could start home-based then branch out. I didn't know. I only knew I needed something other than cooking and cleaning to occupy my time.

If I decided to begin a catering company, I was going to need a website, flyers, business cards, etc. Getting the business off the ground was going to take a lot of time, hard work, and patience. I had the knowledge to do this, but I didn't believe I had the ambition.

***

As we exited the ballpark, I thought about Chandra. I hadn't seen any of my friends in years. After college, I've been the background of Saiaire's foreground. My advice got him the accounts he worked on. I ghostwrote all of his proposals. In essence, I did his work for him. Maybe all I needed was at least one girlfriend to hang with from time to time. Maybe then my life wouldn't be the same tedious routine.

***

It's morning. I was up early looking a hot mess as usual. I had on my red furry robe, my white slippers, and my hair was all over my head. I resembled a crack head begging for loose change.

I'm in the kitchen pouring myself a mug of fresh brewed coffee. Saiaire walked into the kitchen looking sharp as usual. He had on a black long-sleeve button down shirt, a pair of black slacks, black Alligator skinned shoes, and a black tie. He had a thin goatee growing in, and his ponytail was slick back while hanging to the middle of his back. He's 33, but doesn't look a day over 21. I was so lucky to have a man this sweet and beautiful.

"I'm giving the boys a ride this morning."

"Thank you," I said then took a sip of my steaming hot coffee.

"I have a meeting after work. I'll try my hardest to make it home by dinner," Saiaire added as he grabbed a piece of bacon off a plate on the stove.

"That's fine. I'm making pizza's tonight."

"Sounds good. Don't forget take make a personal meat lovers especially for me," Saiaire stated.

"No problem."

Saiaire gave me a hug and a peck on my lips, "Love you babe. You have a good day."

"Love you too. You have a better day,"

Saiaire walked out of the kitchen.

I stared at the plates of bacon and cheese eggs that rested uneaten on the stove. "This is some bullshit!" I screamed out loud. I quit. I'm never making breakfast again. Another meal had gone to waste. What was wrong with my family? All those starving people in Africa would murder us for these two plates of food. These inappreciative bastards consistently allowed good eats to go to waste. I've had it. I've had it. I've had it!

In the mist of my rage, my cell phone rang. This was odd. No one calls me, especially not this early. I stared at my caller ID, 555-0009. Who was this? I answered it. "Hello?"

"Hey you!" Chandra yelled happily.

"Hey Chandra?" I replied while staring at the clock because it is 8:31 a.m.

"Hey Geena! Sorry to call so early. I wanted to catch you before you start your day."

"What's going on?" I asked

"You!" Chandra giggled then continued, "Seriously, what time you have to be at work?"

"I don't work," I said while sitting down on the couch in the living room.

"Damn! You got it made. Anyway, I'm off today and wanted to hook up with you. Is Sai there?"

"Nope. He's at work. Why?"

"No reason. Do you mind having company?"

"Not at all. Give me about an hour to get dressed."

"What is your address?" Chandra asked.

"Oh! Right…It's 3465 Marborn in Lincoln Estates,"

"Okay! See you in about an hour," Chandra blurted then hung up.

I hung up the phone. I was so excited. It's been about two years since I had a friend over to the house and about five years since I've been around a friend without my husband or kids around. I couldn't wait to see her!

***

I immediately ran upstairs to my bedroom. I walked towards the walk-in closet and opened both of the French style doors. I turned my attention to the right side of the closet because that's my side. Umm! What was I going to wear? Something old? Something new? Maybe a mixture of new and old? I didn't know. I hated getting dressed sometimes because I was so indecisive. I stared out of the window. It's a sunny day. Maybe I could wear something that matched the weather. Hmm! A strapless shirt and a pair of capri's should do it!

After an hour, I was completely dressed. I had on a pair of tan khaki style capri's, a tan, white, and orange horizontally striped strapless shirt, and a pair of orange open toed wedge heels. I also had on all of my accessories. They included: my sterling silver chandelier style earrings, my white gold wedding band, my gold charm bracelet, my gold diamond encrusted Rolex, and my gold cross necklace. I was looking good in hopes Chandra would take me somewhere. Maybe we could go to the male review or something of that nature.

As I walked towards the kitchen, I heard my doorbell ring. I cracked a subtle smile as I went to the door to answer it. Chandra stood looking like a super model. She had her sandy-brown hair curly flowing down her back. Her make-up was absolutely flawless. She had on an open back shirt with a "hug-the-body" ankle-length denim shirt with the splits up the side to the knees. Her open toe heels were to die for. I really had to find out where she got them from.

I greeted her as I let her in. While following me to the sitting room, Chandra said, "This is nice. This is really nice. I am so proud of you."

I smiled as I responded, "Thank you. This is mostly a result of Sai's success."

"Well, you know what they say. Behind every good man is a great woman. You are the main contributor to this sweetie," Chandra enlightened.

We walked into the sitting room and sat on the black mink sectional. As we sat down, Chandra sat quietly as she stared at me.

"What?" I nervously asked.

"Nothing. I can't believe that you haven't changed a bit in all of these years. You are truly beautiful," Chandra explained.

"Nah! You're just saying that. Look at you. You look like you should be on television somewhere,"

Chandra crossed her legs towards me, "I know it's early, but do you have anything to drink?"

"Depends on what you want. Girl, we have an entire bar in here. Come on. I'll show you," I offered.

Chandra and I got up from the couch and walked towards the bar. I showed Chandra the entire bar as she was highly impressed. We both fixed ourselves a few drinks while laughing and reminiscing. We took a drink back into the sitting room where we continued our conversation.

"I couldn't believe that at all. You telling me that you are bored? Look at how you living. Look at that fine ass husband of yours," Chandra said.

"I know it sounds weird, but it's true. I am not satisfied at all. I want to try something new; something different. He gave me the okay, so I'm open for suggestions," I explained.

Chandra stared at me again while biting down on her fingernail. This time she was really critiquing my appearance; examining up and down, "Something new hun? You wear lingerie?"

"I have an extensive collection. You wouldn't believe the styles I own," I confessed.

"Do you perform oral?"

"All of the time!" I responded.

"Does he perform oral?" Chandra asked.

"Of course he does. We're married," I took a sip of my drink.

"That doesn't mean anything… Is it any good?"

"Most of the time. The problem is he doesn't stay down there long enough."

Chandra stared at me again. She sat quietly for a moment. I stared into her eyes for a brief second then looked away. Chandra smirked then said, "Have you ever taught him how to please you?"

"I don't understand the question."

"Maybe it would help if you explain to him how to please you."

"Maybe, but I don't want to offend him. I don't want to make him feel like he doesn't know what he is doing."

"From what you're complaining about, he doesn't. Before you can tell him how to please you, you have to know how to please you. Do you know how to please you?" Chandra said then took another sip of her drink.

"Of course," I said with a confused expression on my face.

"Well, tell me. How can someone please you Geena?" Chandra boldly asked.

I sat quietly for a couple of seconds. That was a weird question for another woman to ask me. I have never been asked anything like this before. Now that I thought about it, I really didn't know the answer to Chandra's question. I knew I liked it passionate, freaky, and sensual, but that's about it. What would make me climb the walls? What would turn me on to the extreme? I was seriously going to have to ponder this question a bit.

Chandra slid closer to me glaring into my face. Thigh touched my thigh. She smirked in response to my silence leaning towards me. She slowly licked her lips, "Hmm!" She downed the last swallow of her drink then continued, "Have you ever tried a woman?"

I paused, "No."

Chandra glanced down at my cleavage then stared into my eyes, "Have you thought about trying a woman?"

This liquor was getting to me because for some reason the way she looked at me was turning me on, "I've fantasized about it once or twice."

Chandra placed her hand upon my thigh. I stared down at her hand then into her eyes. She said, "Do you wanna find out what it's like?"

I took a gulp of my drink and inhaled and exhaled slowly. I pierced the clock with my eyes. It read 11:02 a.m. I stared at Chandra's full lips then into her beautiful eyes. I said, "I'm a married woman."

"That's not answering my question," Chandra took my drink out of my hand and sat it on the coffee table. She slid extremely close to me placing her hand on my thigh inside the panty line. She stared me in my eyes with her face about six inches from mine. I felt a strong sexual tension between us. I stared at her lips again. She said, "Do you?"

I thought of the dream I had several nights ago. I closed my eyes and had a flash of the woman behind me holding my breast as she kissed my neck. I opened my eyes, "Even if I did, I'm a married woman."

Chandra drew in near and gave me a peak on my lips. I was stunned as I stared at her. Her face was only two inches away from mine; I could feel her breath on my cheek. She said, "So your marriage is holding you back from something you obviously desire?"

"Yes…I can't cheat on him. He's too good to me and the boys."

Chandra smirked, "You've always been the good girl. Aren't you tired of that? You know deep down inside you want to be naughty. Be naughty for once. He doesn't have to know, and if wants, he's free to join in."

I paused for a spell sitting in a state of silence. Recalling my dream, did I dream this up? This could not be real. I've always fantasized about having a three-some but didn't ever think the opportunity would present itself, especially with someone as gorgeous as Chandra; the very woman that gave me my first kiss in high school, freshman year, before I met Sai. She was sexually active but I was not. She taught me how to kiss preparing me for my first time.

I turned to her as she rubbed the back of her hand gently across the side of my face, "I've never been with a woman. I don't know what I'm doing."

"I'll show you", Chandra kissed me passionately while rubbing the back of my neck along my hairline. I placed my hand on top of her breast as I ran my other hand up and down her back. She tilted my head up and back as she massaged my neck with her tongue and lips; going up and down one side, across then up and down the other as I gripped her shoulders. The feeling was indescribable; she turned me on more than my husband did.

I pulled away from her. Chandra said, "What?"

"I can't do this. I'm not a lesbian. I love dick. I love my husband."

"I'm not a lesbian either. I have a boyfriend. If it'll make you feel more comfortable, we can do this with Sai."

I frowned. The thought of another woman touching my husband didn't sit well with me, especially someone as gorgeous as Chandra. What if she's better than me? What if my husband preferred to have sex with her instead of me?

This was something I definitely had to think about. I wanted to spice up our boring sex life, and I did often fantasize about a three-some, but I'm unsure if it should remain a fantasy or should it be acted upon. I said, "I'll have to think about that."

Chandra grabbed my jewel and immediately started rubbing my clit up and down. Before I could respond, she bit my neck so hard, yet it felt so good, as she rubbed my clit up and down with the side of her knuckle applying more and more pressure. I tilted my head back breathing hard trying not to moan. My mind said to push her away and make her leave but damn this felt good. I opened my legs as she climbed on top of me sliding in between them. She continued biting and sucking my neck as she rubbed my clit. I gripped the side of her trunk as she kissed my lips passionately. I felt like I was going to explode. She placed her hand inside of my capri's feeling my moisture. She rubbed my clit up and down then removed her fingers. She stopped kissing me; staring intently into my eyes then she sucked my moisture off of her fingers mumbling in the most sensual sounding voice, "You taste good."

Chandra slid down my body with her knees onto the carpet yanking my capri's and underwear off simultaneously. I leaned back on the sofa with my arms folded back gripping the frame as she licked and kissed up my inner right thigh, took a sip of me then kissed down my left thigh to my knee. She stopped then slowly removed my left heel. She cuffed my foot with both of her hands massaging the sole with her thumbs in circular motions. She slowly and gently sucked up my big toe then slowly moved her wet tongue between each toe in a circular motion. I squirmed something fierce tightly gripping the frame of the sofa feeling vibrations flow throughout my body, especially from my jewel as it deeply pulsated. I shouted, "Shhhiiiittttt!" I couldn't believe how this woman was making my body feel. Sai had never sucked my toes like this.

On her knees with her hands on my thighs, she pierced my eyes with hers with the most lustful expression I had ever seen. She stood as she rubbed her hands up my thighs staring lustfully into my eyes. As she rubbed up, she gently spread my legs and licked up my vaginal split. I released a loud moan. With her index fingers, she split my lips sticking her tongue in and out of my vagina then moving it in circular motions as she went in and out. She injected three of her fingers going in and out slowly as she caressed my g-spot staring intently into my eyes. As she finger fucked me applying more and more pressure to my g-spot, she tongue kissed my clit; eating it like she hadn't had dinner for a few days and was starving. She applied more and more pressure to my g-spot with her fingers as she injected in and out faster and faster while continuously sucking, blowing, and licking my clit. I shouted,

"Uh….Shit…Yes….Yes…Got damn." My entire body exploded as I moved so much I now lain on the sofa as Chandra chased me with her fingers and tongue.

Suddenly my legs locked tightly around her head. I could barely breathe as I quickly sat up. Chandra removed her fingers but kept sucking on my clit. My waist trembled and before I knew it my entire body was trembling as I kept cumming and cumming back to back feeling it throughout my entire body. She just kept going and going as I screamed in pleasure hoping my neighbors did not hear me. My entire body was jerking and trembling; I couldn't take anymore. I pushed her head away and said, "I can't take anymore." She pulled away from me.

I covered my eyes with both of my hands and cried. I just had the most mind-blowing multiple full body orgasm; actually I've never had a full body orgasm let alone multiple. Chandra lain on top of me gently rubbing the side of my face. She said, "Are you okay?" I was speechless. I rubbed my eyes and didn't say one word. She kissed me then rubbed her hands through my hair. I didn't say one word as I wondered how I let this happen. My husband was all I ever knew about sex. He was my first and only until now. I just cheated on him. I really didn't know how I felt about this situation. Chandra just fucked the shit out of me and damn that orgasm felt good as hell. My body needed that, but this was wrong. It was so wrong. My husband would never cheat on me…or would he? Either way, with how she just fucked me, I could only imagine what she would do to Sai. No…No…We couldn't have this three-some. As bad as it sounds, I wanted to keep her all to myself.

Chandra kissed me passionately. I leaned up and told her to move. She obliged. I stood and walked towards the stairs. Chandra was on the sofa still on her hands and knees. I said, "Come on." She got up from the sofa and came to me. I grabbed her hand and walked her up stairs. We did it again and again. I was addicted.

***

I stood in the shower allowing the warm water to massage my back as I gently rubbed the side of my neck as I tilted my head to the left side; I inhaled and exhaled slowly. I tilted my head back into the flowing stream of water allowing it to saturate my hair and drizzle down my face. I held one hand across my chest hugging my breast as I sighed seeing flashes of Chandra's lustful gaze. I felt a deep sense of guilt flowing through me. Although being with Chandra was amazing, I just cheated on my husband. How could I look him in his eyes? Should I tell him? I always fantasized about being the naughty girl, but after being naughty, I actually felt terrible about it. I had to wash the scent of Chandra off of me although my mind and body could never erase the moment we had.

***

Several hours had passed, and I was back into my reality; five sons and their friends tearing through my house like little Tasmanian Devils driving me half insane with all of the ruckus, and Sai?…Working late at the office as usual.

As I washed the dishes, my cell phone rang. I dried my hand by rubbing it against my jeans, pulled it from its holder, and stared at the caller I.D. It was Chandra. I pressed "ignore" and returned it to its case that rested upon my belt. She called back two more times but I allowed it to ring and go to voicemail. I took a cigarette from my apron pocket, placed it between my lips, and was about to spark it when Sai walked into the kitchen. I quickly removed the cigarette returning it to my apron pocket and laying my yellow lighter onto the counter next to the sink. I stared at my husband. His beautiful eyes and full soft lips with that long beautiful hair of his pulled back into the usual ponytail. He said, "How was your day?"

"Interesting. Yours?"

"The usual headache."

I walked to my husband and gave him the most endearing hug. He embraced me as he gently kissed my neck. I slowly pulled away from the hug staring intently into his eyes. While holding onto my lower back, he said, "Is everything okay?"

I rubbed the top of his head sliding down the back of his head. I slid his ponytail holder off tossing it to the floor. I stared my husband in his eyes as I combed his hair with my fingers. I didn't know if it's the result of guilt or if I wanted to prove something to myself, but I wanted to rip my husband's clothes off and fuck him in this kitchen…but the kids were here. The kids are always here.

I said, "Let's be naughty."

Sai smirked, "What do you mean?"

"Fuck me, right here, right now."

Sai pulled me towards him as we stood hip to hip, "Umm…I would love to, but what if the kids catch us?"

"I'm willing to take that chance. We don't have to take nothing off."

Sai glanced into the living room as we both heard the kids bumbling about, "Let's go upstairs and lock the door."

My shoulders slumped, "Never mind Sai." I walked away from him.

Sai stood with a baffled expression upon his face as he distressingly ran his hands through his hair. He leaned onto the counter resting his elbow on it while cuffing the side of his face with his hand, "What is wrong with you?"

I turned towards him speaking sternly as I clinched my teeth together trying not to be too loud, "You…You are what's wrong with me. Why can't you be impulsive sometimes?"

He stood up straight with his hands pressed against the counter top, "Impulsive? Since when do you want impulsive?"

"Since now. I'm bored as fuck Sai. Why can't my fantasies be real? Why do I have to continuously comply with your wishes? What about what I want?"

"What do you want?...a divorce hmmm? I bust my ass every day to supply you and the boys with a life to die for…"

I interrupted him, "Who asked for that?" I glanced around the kitchen then continued, "I don't recall ever asking for *any* of this. This lifestyle you claim is to die for is the lifestyle *you* want. I never had a say and still don't."

"That's not true and you know it."

"Do I? Because most of the time I feel like I'm suffocating inside. I want some excitement. I want a life too. All I asked is for you to fuck me…fuck me real good. You won't even give me that. I sit here all day long bored out of my mind. I spend so much time alone I don't even know how to act in social situations. This house…this lifestyle…everything you want…has become my prison."

Sai rubbed his nose with his index finger and thumb then rubbed his chin. He inhaled slowly then exhaled quickly, "So what now? Do you want a divorce?"

I slowly closed my eyes tightly then opened them as I felt tears filling, "No…I love you."

"I love you too," he approached me embracing me tightly, "I'm trying to make you happy. I didn't realize you weren't. Just tell me what to do and I'll do it."

I gently touched my husband's face with my hands rubbing down his cheeks towards his chin, "Don't make love to me…fuck me…fuck me real good."

I jammed my hand into his pants pulling out his penis. I placed my thumb along the nerve underneath his penis and proceeded to jacking him off. Sai breathed hard as he stared into my eyes. I got down on my knees wrapping my lips around the head of his penis as I moved my tongue in circular motions. Sai rubbed his fingers through my hair. I placed the tip of my tongue along the nerve and sucked in and out, in and out, Sai pulled my hair then said, "Stop, stop. The kids are here."

I peered up at him as I stood. He put his penis back into his pants. I quietly walked away as he grabbed a hold of my arm stopping me. He said, "We'll finish this later, okay?"

"No, you finish it later. Until you fuck me the way I want to be fucked, I'm not sleeping with you anymore."

"Look you are my wife and I love you. I don't feel comfortable treating you like a slut because you're not one. You're a good, virtuous woman. Why would you want me to treat you like a slut?"

"Haven't you heard the saying, 'a lady in public a freak in the bed'? Maybe I wanna be the freak in the bed. Maybe I want to experience the thrill of possibly getting caught." I shook my head in disapproval, "See how much time we wasted. You could have already fucked the shit out of me by now. Look at how long we've been in here and not one time has any of the boys come in here. I'm going to bed Sai. You clean up after them." I walked out of the kitchen.

***

I laid in bed with my back towards my husband on my right side facing the window. The curtains were pulled open as I glared at the full moon. I didn't know what was happening to me. Was I going through some type of mid-life crisis? Was I happy here? I wasn't happy here. I was used to being here.

My cell phone rang. I reached over to the nightstand and grabbed it. I answered so quickly as not to awaken Sai that I did not get a chance to see who was calling. I whispered, "Hello."

Chandra said, "You're ignoring me now? I called you three times today."

I sat up on the edge of the bed, "What do you expect from me? What do you want me to say?"

"I don't want you to say or do anything. I want you to be you. Be my friend."

"Hold on," I slipped my slippers on and walked out of the bedroom. I sat on the top step with my back against the wall, "I have a husband and have to get up early in the morning. What is it you want?"

"I don't know. For you to ignore me after what we had, makes me feel some kind of way."

"What kind of way?"

"Not a good feeling."

"I don't mean to make you feel that way. It's just…difficult for me to take in."

"Look, I'm not a lesbian. I'm not trying to break up your marriage or have you run away with me; nothing that dramatic. I just feel there's nothing wrong with having benefits to this friendship."

"I need time to think."

Sai said, "Think about what?"

I felt a deep sense of nervousness as I thought he was asleep. I handed him the phone. He said, "Hello."

Chandra said, "Hey Sai…You remember me?"

"Who is this?"

"Chandra from high school."

Sai smiled, "Hey girl. How have you been?"

"I've been good. You have a lovely family, and I'm so proud of all you have accomplished."

"Well thank you. How has life treated you?"

"I can't complain…hey…did your wife tell you?"

"Tell me what?"

As soon as I heard Sai say that, my heartbeat hastened and my hands trembled a bit. I had no idea what Chandra was about to say to him. Would she tell him about us? Oh God.

"We were planning something very special for your birthday."

"Really?"

"Yes, trust me…You will *love* this gift. I hope you're open-minded."

"Mostly."

"Well good. I can't wait to see you again."

"Me too. Why don't you stop by here tomorrow night? We all can have some drinks and catch up. Seems you and Geena already caught up."

My heart sunk into my stomach. I was just about to tell Chandra that we had to end these benefits because I needed to work on my marriage. Now this fool just invited her over. This was not good at all. I felt the need to tell him everything, but how would that make him feel? That would insult his pride as a man that I turned to a woman to please me sexually, and I didn't officially turn to her; she took it. I couldn't believe this was happening.

"Sounds good. You have a good night and here's Geena," Sai handed me the phone.

I held the phone in my hand for a spell. I stared at Sai and said, "What did she say to you?"

"Nothing, told me about a surprise for my birthday. Why?"

"I wanted it to be a surprise. Good night."

Sai smirked, "Good night." He walked away.

I put the phone to my ear, "I don't appreciate you telling my husband about a surprise I hadn't planned for him."

"Lighten up. You know good and well you want that. Stop fighting your urges. Your fantasies will be fulfilled."

"I don't want to do that anymore."

"Sure you don't. Good Night. I'll see you tomorrow," she hung up.

I sat in silence; stunned. This woman had lost her mind. She couldn't force me to have a three-some with her and my husband.

***

I stood in my kitchen after dropping the boys off at school. My eyes were puffy because I barely got a wink of sleep last night. I kept thinking about Chandra. I wondered what she was up to and why she wants this three-some so badly. Did she want my husband? What was really going on with her and would she tell Sai about us? I wished I hadn't done it. I wished I could rewind that day. Why did I tell her about my sexual dissatisfaction? By doing so, I invited her to do what she did. Never tell anyone that you are not sexually satisfied because that leaves room for them to creep on in. I had no idea she would do that. I was not expecting to sleep with her when I invited her over. However, I couldn't erase the day nor could I erase how much I enjoyed it. The guilt within me was insurmountable. I wondered if I should tell Sai and what consequences that would have on my marriage. I loved my husband with everything in me, and yes, I was insatiably attracted to him and would never leave him no matter what, but this would probably be the end of my marriage.

I wished Chandra would go away and never return. That would certainly be a blessing. All I could think about was what was to come later on today. How could I sit in the same room with her and Sai and behave as nothing happened between us? What she gives me that look? That damn near irresistible 'come hither' stare? Would Sai notice? Would he question? I'm not even sure if Sai would be down with a three-some, and I'm not sure if I want Chandra getting her hands on my husband. I'd probably flip out as soon as she touched him and he enjoyed it. I'm driving myself half-crazy with all of these unanswered questions.

***

Daylight came quickly as I was as nervous as a woman on the run meeting with a Federal Marshall; knowing yet not knowing what would transpire. I cooked and cleaned as usual and took the boys to school. Sai left without eating anything more than a piece of bacon as usual, but the boys surprised me by eating all of their breakfast. That made me smile inside. My youngest son said, "Mom, you're the best cook ever." It tickled my soul.

I sat on the couch looking like a bum with my baggy blue sweats on, silk scarf concealing my hair, my leather slippers, and a tank top. I sat on the sofa in the sitting room staring at the television. I was watching television but it seemed the television watched me. Flashes of Chandra and I kissing came to mind. As I glanced around the sofa, a flash of her biting my neck came to mind. I rubbed my eyes with the palms of my hands wishing I could erase everything that I could erase everything that happened but could not.

My cell phone rang loudly startling me. I grabbed it from lying next to me on the sofa and checked the caller I.D. It was Chandra. My first mind said, "Don't answer it", but I had a bone to pick with her. I answered the phone, "Hello,"

"Hey you. I'm outside. Unlock the door."

"I'm not unlocking the door, and I'm not letting you in."

Chandra breathed deeply into the phone then said, "Why are you acting like this?"

"I don't appreciate you telling my husband about a surprise. I'm not having a three-some with you and him. You're not touching my husband."

Chandra snickered, "You think I want Sai?"

"Do you?"

"No baby...The only one I want is you. If I have to share you to have you, so be it."

"I thought you said you weren't a lesbian."

"I'm not. I already told you that I have a boyfriend."

"Well, I guess I'm not the only one sexually unsatisfied, hunh?"

"No man can satisfy me. I'm bisexual and have to have my cake and eat it too. You're my cake, and I'm ready to eat."

"What are you not understanding? I am a married woman. I love my husband and have never planned on being with you in anyway including sexually."

Chandra paused, breathing deeply on the phone for a spell then said, "Well, you sure weren't thinking about your husband when we fucked four times; three of which in *your* husband's bed. The passion you had…you can't tell me you didn't enjoy it as much as I did. You can't tell me you didn't like the way I suck on that pussy."

I pulled the phone away from my ear shaking my head in disapproval. How could I rebuttal that? It was true, "I did enjoy it. I enjoyed it so much that it made me realize how wrong it truly was. I need to work on my marriage and don't need your assistance to do so."

"Hmmm…Okay. Whatever you want momma. I'll see you this evening," she hung up.

I immediately called her back. She picked up on the second ring, "Hey."

"Are you going to tell my husband?"

"Do you want me to tell your husband?"

"That's so foul."

"You started it."

"How so?"

"I had no plans on telling Sai shit but I could. You open the door, let me get that pussy or I'll run my mouth like diarrhea."

"You're threatening me?"

"I don't make threats. That's a plan. You know good and well the chemistry we had was real. You made love to me, and I made love to you...repeatedly. What Sai doesn't know can't kill him."

"I can't Chandra and should not have the first time. My husband doesn't deserve this."

"Well, that's your issue to deal with. I'm horny, and I'm horny for you. Now, let me in and let me eat that pussy."

"You're black mailing me."

"I'm giving you what you want."

I pulled the phone away from my ear. I saw a flash of Chandra between my legs as they trembled uncontrollably. I felt my body tingle as I remembered that mind-blowing orgasm. I felt stuck. I felt so stuck because this was so wrong, but I couldn't allow her to tell him. I wished I had never done it.

I put the phone back to my ear, "If I do it, will this be the last time?"

"If you want it to be, but I doubt you'd want it to. This will save your marriage. You still get to have your gorgeous husband, and you get to be fucked the way you want to be fucked. It's a win-win situation for the both of us."

"Promise me you won't tell Sai about this."

"I promise. As far as he knows, we're best friends."

I paused staring at the front door, "Okay. I'm about to unlock the door."

I hung up and walked towards the front door. I unlocked it and walked towards the bar. I was going to need a stiff one for this. I poured a double shot of Vodka and quickly ingested it. I felt it burn as it went down but I didn't think that would be enough. I poured another double shot, and as I inhaled, Chandra walked in. She was dressed down. Sharp opened toed stilettos with the silver gun for a heel laced up to the mid thigh. She has on a short black skirt that hugged her hips and behind perfectly with a black body hugging shirt with the back out. Her slanted eyes had the smoky-eyed look as I could smell her perfume from across the room. She said, "Even looking rough you're still fine as hell."

I sat the glass down on the bar and turned towards her. I could feel the liquor kicking in. Chandra slowly walked towards me as I stared into her eyes. She licked her full, silky looking lips and bit down the bottom slowly sucked it and released. I did not know or understand why because I had never had a sexual attraction towards women before, but this woman was irresistible.

She stood in front of me as she slid my scarf off of my head dropping it onto the marble tiled floor. She ran her fingers through the sides of my hair as she gently, passionately kissed my lips. I tried not to touch her much but couldn't help placing my hands upon her shoulders. She hugged me tightly as we kissed with her arms below mine rubbing along my back. Without hesitation, she shoved her hand into my pants feeling my moisture rubbing up and down slowly. I breathed hard for a few seconds then kissed her neck. I wanted to bite her neck up to her ears, but with those heels on, she was taller than me.

Chandra pulled away from me as she took her shirt off revealing a red laced bra and her chiseled abs. She had a body to die for; the perfect hourglass frame, thick in all the right places – almost made me want to start hitting the gym. I rubbed my hand down the middle of her stomach area while sucking on my bottom lip. Chandra pulled my shirt off of me as my breast hung freely because I wasn't wearing a bra. Chandra grabbed my left breast with both of her hands licking my nipple with the fast flick of her tongue as I watched while pulling her hair.

"What the hell is this?"

I glanced up and saw Sai standing in the doorway wearing a blue silk button down shirt, some tan slacks, and some brown leather shoes. My heart almost stopped as Chandra turned towards him smirking. I was speechless as he slowly drew near us.

"I…I…" I couldn't even attempt to find the words to explain this. I was caught.

"If I knew you were into this, we could have done this a long time ago," Sai said as he unbuttoned his shirt lustfully glancing between Chandra and I.

I was stunned as I stood with my back against the bar frozen. Sai tossed his shirt onto the pool table revealing his perfectly sculpted chest and chiseled abs. His body looked like a sculpture. Chandra went to him and unbuttoned his pants. She pulled out his pole as it was fully erect ready to do some damage. She slid her hand across it, caressing it with her thumb and index fingers as Sai stared intently into my eyes. She got down on her knees wrapping her full lips around my husband's piece. Watching her suck him, turned me on more than anything I had ever imagined. I slid my pants off and went towards them. I rubbed my hand across the left side of his chest as I leaned in for a kiss. Sai tilted his head down kissing me passionately as he caressed my breasts with his hands. He moved his hands down placing them in between my southern set of lips. He rubbed up and down then stuck his fingers inside of me. He finger fucked me until Chandra made him cum.

Still hard, he picked me up holding by my behind shoving his pole inside of me as he walked me towards the pool table. He laid me on top of the pool table with my legs hanging off gripping my waist as he long-stroked me. With every thrust, he smacked the g-spot perfectly making me howl in pleasure.

Chandra climbed on top of the pool table from the other end. She leaned down kissing me as Sai fucked the shit out of me in a way that was unfamiliar to my being. Chandra sucked on my nipples as my body exploded with foreign pleasure. I shouted, "Got damn...fuck me...fuck me...shhhiiiittttt!."

Sai stroked me fast and hard as Chandra sat on my face riding it. I sucked and licked her juices as Sai served me cumming inside of me, but it wasn't over. We fucked all around the entire house. Needless to say, I had the most amazing, breath-taking, and mind-blowing orgasms I had ever experienced. From that day forth, we included Chandra in a lot of our sexual escapades. We stayed married, our sex life was explosive, and we had a new toy.

Justice

Introduction

His abs rippled like mountains as a thin hairline ran down the middle like a river carving into a valley. The dim lights in this office was reminiscent to candle lights on a lighter, less orange scale bouncing off of his chest making his perfectly, toned, athletic build seem fantastical; a figment of my imagination. I always fantasized about being naughty but never had the courage to do so. I have no feelings attached. I do not love this man. I do not even know his name. All I know is he's beautiful in every way imaginable, and I want him; right here, right now.

His deep, smooth sounding smoky voice mumbled, "I aim to please."

I removed my red suit jacket tossing it onto the floor as I sat on top of my large twenty person table in the conference room. I took the tip of my heel and slipped my shoes off one at a time as he stared intensely into my eyes. I could see his definition through his slacks as his piece rested down his right leg trying to burst out; my goodness – this man was blessed. My clit throbbed a bit anticipating him entering me.

He came towards me lifting my chin up with his bent index finger softly kissing my lips. We kissed passionately for what felt like a few minutes although it was actually a matter of seconds as I gently bit down on his lip sucking it. I pulled away running my fingers across his chest as I bit down on his shoulder. He ran his hands up my skirt grabbing me with his fingers underneath my ass and his thumb strumming down the middle of my vaginal lips. I dripped profusely as my juices saturated the inside of his hand. I unsnapped my skirt as he snatched it off. I unbuttoned and unzipped his grey slacks as his piece popped right on out welcoming me.

He grabbed it placing it against my clit moving it in circular motions absorbing some of my wetness. I grabbed his shoulders tightly trying not to moan so as we don't get caught in this conference room. He rubbed his piece up and down my valley, slowly taking a condom out of his pocket with the other hand. He tore open the condom while staring into my eyes, slipped it on, then slipped into me.

I gasped, unable to breathe the moment he shoved it in. He had so much girth he may have stretched my walls – my pussy never felt so full. My walls hugged his penis like a fitted leather glove as he stroked in an out slowly at first but gradually picking up pace – he went slow then fast, fast then slow, long-stroke to short-stroke; trying not to scream, but I screamed relentlessly.

"Justice...Justice," Melvin said.

Justice stared out of the large window in a daze. Jordan tapped her shoulder, "Boss lady," she pointed towards the speaker.

"Yes," Justice said as she quickly came down from her fantasy into reality. She was in a meeting in the conference room.

Melvin smiled revealing his straight perfectly white teeth, "The advice column."

"Aw...Sorry my mind is somewhere else this morning. Would you please repeat?"...

Something New

"How can we get these books into the hands of customers? That's the objective of this meeting," Justice stated as she walked towards the projector.

Robert raised his hand.

"Yes!" Justice said.

"We've put together a great media kit. The sales have increased."

"By what margin? 1%? 2%? I want an increase of at least 10%. I am in business to make money, not crumbs. We need a better, more effective media kit for this book campaign. We are being paid for a service. It's our duty to provide the best and nothing less. Sorry, but we'll be here all night unless we come up with a plan," Justice explained.

"I have to go to my son's soccer tournament. It's the last game of the season, and I've already missed the entire season," Mike blurted.

"Fine! Go!" Justice said with an attitude.

Mike got up from the table. He grabbed his things from the desk and walked out of the room. Justice turned the projector off then turned the lights back on, "Now, turn to page 4 of the campaign plan."

Everybody in the room turned to page 4 of their campaign plan. Posie spoke, "I believe we should contact motion picture companies. This novel will make a great movie."

Justice tapped her pen against her hand while pacing back and forth. She stopped, "That's a good idea. Posie get on that first thing Monday morning."

"Will do," Posie agreed.

Justice stared at the clock on the wall in the conference room. The time was 7:15 p.m. She had been at work since 6 o'clock a.m. She was tired, "Damn! Another 12+ hour day," she mumbled to herself.

"What was that Justice? I didn't hear you," Jerome asked.

"You weren't supposed to," Justice stated then continued, "Wrap it up everybody. Go home and have a great weekend."

"What? The meeting isn't over. We didn't discuss the campaign plan. You just said we're going to be here all night until we can come up with a plan," Posie blurted.

Mark mumbled, "Shut up!"

"I know what I said. Time...you all have good comprehension. Read it over the weekend and return with an individual plan," Justice replied.

"Bet! I still have time to catch the game. I'm out!" Mark screamed as he grabbed his folders and exited the room in a hurry.

"Are you okay Justice? You never close in the middle of a meeting," Jerome questioned in concern.

"I'm okay. Don't worry about me. You have you a good weekend Jerome."

"I will and thank you. I haven't had a free day since I started," Jerome confessed.

"Sorry about that."

"Don't be. You're a great boss, and this is a good company," Jerome said as he grabbed his briefcase and walked out of the conference room.

Justice gave a subtle smirk nodding her head in gratitude. She unplugged the projector.

Posie walked towards her, "Justice, what's really going on?"

"I don't know. I'm having some kind of late-20's crisis. All I do is work and sleep. Even in my dreams I'm working. I don't have a life. I feel like I'm missing out on some important experiences," Justice admitted.

Danni said, "You ain't missing shit." She walked out.

Justice and Posie glanced at her.

Jordan joined the conversation, "Yes you do boss. You are a young sistah who owns a multi-million dollar business. You should be proud of yourself."

"I am, but that's not what I mean. I work so much that I don't have time for anything else. My little sister is 24, and she's getting married next weekend. I'm 29…no man, no kids…I have nothing," Justice added.

Posie replied, "That's her life not yours. You're different. You have a vision and a dream. Without people like you, people like me wouldn't have a job."

Jordan jumped in, "Besides, there's plenty of men that would be interested in a beautiful, intelligent, independent woman such as you. Surprised you're not getting you back blown out every night."

Justice shook her head in disapproval, "You two are missing the point. I don't have the time to meet anyone to have a life to experience anything. My biological clock is ticking, and I don't have the time to fall in love…I haven't been touched in 4 years."

Posie and Jordan simultaneously scream, "Damn!"

"That's a damn shame boss. That shit is clearly unethical. You got some toys?" Jordan said.

"Tell me about it!" Justice said as she pulled the podium to the corner of the room to get it out of the walkway.

"Look, I don't know how you get down, but tomorrow I can take you out somewhere," Jordan offered.

"Take me out? Like to a club?" Justice asked.

"Yeah, but I promise you ain't seen nothing like this."

"So, *you* are going to hook me up with a man? You don't know my type."

"Oh! There's a man for every woman's type."

Posie asked, "Where is this club, and why have you withheld this information from me?"

"It's a secret. However, if y'all want to go, I can pick the both of you up no later than 9 p.m. tomorrow night," Jordan said.

"I'm in. Shit, I have nothing to lose except more lonely nights," Justice calmly stated.

"Count me in as well," Posie blurted.

"Okay! I will see you ladies tomorrow night," Jordan said as she walked out of the conference room.

Posie shut down the three computers behind the conference desk. Justice turned the lights off then she and Posie both exited the building.

***

Justice walked into her luxurious two-bedroom condo. As soon as she stepped into her condo, she was happily greeted by her female golden retriever, Poose. Justice knelt down to embrace her dog, "Hey Poose. Hey girl." She rubbed the dog's head. Poose jumped up and down excited to see her master.

Justice removed her suit jacket tossing it across the back of her crème colored Italian leather sectional. She quickly unbuttoned the top three buttons on her blouse and took off her heels. She walked to her answering machine and checked her messages, "You have seven new messages. To hear your messages, press 1." Justice pressed the number 1 button. The first message played, "Justice, this is Greg. Give me a call back at 555-5678. Talk to you later."

Justice smirked and said, "Never. I wonder how you got my number loser. Stay at home with your wife."

The next message played, "Jus, did you see the news girl? Some man was murdered in the park. I tell you this world has gone mad. Niggas are ill these days. Call me when you get this."

While flipping through the stack of mail next to the answering machine, "Momma, get a life. I don't care about some strange man getting murdered."

The next message played, "Justice, this Sayshawn the baby brother you never call. Anyway, I need to borrow $300. My baby momma tripping again. Hit me up asap."

Justice swung punches in the air, "Use a damn condom and get a job! Stop making babies you can't take care of! Birth control works you spoiled brat. Man up."

The next message played, "Jus, this Demetrius. I've recently self-published another novel. I need a publicity campaign to market it. Give me a call back, so we can discuss your services. I can be reached at 555-2938."

While grabbing the television remote from the coffee table and turning on her 62" LCD television, "You suck. Your books are poorly edited, boring as hell, have no plot, and only make sense to you. I cannot market your book if I paid someone to buy it."

Justice plopped down on the sectional. Poose lain down on the floor next to where Justice sat. The next message played, "Justice, this is the original Justice. (He giggled) Give me a call when you can baby girl."

"Mr. Justice Moorse. My daddy. The man I'm named after. I'll call you tomorrow."

The next message played, "Justice, You forgot to pick me up today."

While flipping through the channels on the television, "Fuck! How did I forget to pick my niece up from drill team?"

Justice jumped up grabbing the cordless phone from the table next to the answering machine. She turned the answering machine off and dialed her big sister's phone number. It rang twice. "Mariah, I am so sorry," Justice frantically apologized.

"It's okay Jus. Meechie's daddy picked her up," Mariah calmly stated.

"Is she there? I want to apologize."

"Nope. This is Friday night girl. She is gone. You know she got a little social life now. She won't be back home until Sunday afternoon," Mariah enlightened.

"Okay, please let her know that I am so sorry."

"I will."

"Bye."

Justice hung the phone up feeling terrible about forgetting to pick up her niece. She walked towards the kitchen. She bypassed the refrigerator and went straight to the bar. She walked behind the bar grabbing a bottle of brown liquor. She poured it into a chilled glass and sat down at the bar.

She was deep in thought: *This really sucks. I'm at home alone with nothing to do on a weekend. I only have one friend, and she lives across the globe in London. I don't have anyone to call, and I am bored out of my mind. I am horny. This is so crazy. I have a company worth 5.3 million dollars, and I am completely alone. Hell, even ugly people got somebody. I don't have anybody. Greg? What a joke? I gave him five years of my life for him to marry the woman he cheated on me with. Now that I'm out here doing the damn thing, he wants to call. With the way he treated me, I hope he doesn't hold his breath waiting for my return call. My sister Mariah is the only person who could have given him my new number. She's always talking about lowering my standards. I'm sorry, but I know what type of man I want to be with. I'm not settling just so I won't have to sit here alone. Also, I work between 12 and 16 hours a day. I often bring my work home with me. I don't have the time to spend with someone to get to know him. Hell, I don't have the time to get out and meet anybody. I don't ask for much. I don't need a rich man. I want somebody who has some degree of intelligence, ambitious, charming, charismatic, good sense of humor, attractive, and sensitive. Most of the men I've met out here today fall into one of three categories: 1) Treat you good, but want to live off of you. 2) Paid, but treat you like shit. 3) Broke and treat you like shit. I don't have the time.*

Justice downed her shot of liquor. She let it settle in her system for a few seconds then she poured another drink. She continued with her thought process:

I am so horny, but I don't want to be a whore because I'm not one and never have been. However, Tyvid might actually be correct. In my case, fucking would be the best thing. I don't have time for a relationship, but I am a woman who has needs. A sexual relationship would be good. I don't have to worry about any complaining about lack of quality time. I don't have to worry about not having dinner ready, etc. I only wish I had someone to call specifically for that.

Justice's cell phone rang. She unclipped her Galaxy examining the caller I.D. "Who the hell is this?" She said aloud. She answered the phone, "Hello?"

"What up boss? You dressed yet?" Jordan screamed in the phone over the music playing in the background.

"I thought you said we were going out tomorrow," Justice reminded.

"Nah! I was talking about going out tomorrow with Posie. We are going out tonight girl."

"You didn't want Posie to come with us?" Justice questioned then inhaled her second shot.

"Hell nah! She is too uppity to go where we going."

"We aren't going to a gutter spot are we? I'm not trying to have my Benz jacked, and I'm definitely not trying to fight anyone," Justice explained.

"Hell nah! I don't roll like that. This spot is a little different. Posie? I doubt if she fit in this world. Just get dressed, give me your address, and I'll be to get you in an hour."

"All right. 66897 Kings Hwy."

"Damn! You ballin' in the Estates. I see you."

"What do you think? I own the company, and I pay you $40,000 a year. You're only one of twelve employees," Justice said while giggling.

"I'll be there."

Justice hung up the phone. She screamed, "Yes! I am going to kick it! I'm going to kick it!" She ran into the living room and jumped up and down on the sectional. Poose got so excited she ran around the room in circles barking.

Justice grabbed the remote control to her large floor model stereo system and turned it on. She blasted some R&B tracks from her mix CD. She ran upstairs to the master bedroom. Poose followed behind her.

Justice went in her walk in closet staring at her wardrobe. She wanted to wear something inviting, but not anything sleezy. She grabbed her low-rise medium denim hip huggers from the hanger. She grabbed her spaghetti strap black satin shirt. She pulled her black pat and leather looking open toed heels out of the shoebox.

She took a quick shower then put her clothes on. She put on light make-up that completely blended with her medium brown complexion. She put on her 1ct diamond earrings, her ladies white gold Christian Dior watch, and her two white gold diamond rings that she wore on both of her middle fingers on both hands. She sprayed on a fragrance called Beautiful and sprayed oil sheen on her low tapered Halle Berry styled haircut. She looked like a million bucks.

As soon as Justice walked downstairs, her doorbell rang. She glanced at the clock. Only 45 minutes had passed. She opened the door. Jordan and another woman stood there. She let them in.

"Damn! Justice. This is nice as fuck. It's like something on MTV Cribs on a smaller scale," Jordan confessed as she looked around.

"Thank you. You want a drink?"

"Sure. By the way, this is my *friend* Dominica. She's going out with us tonight," while looking over at Dominica, "This is my boss and friend Justice."

While extending her hand for Justice to shake, she said, "Nice to meet you. You have a beautiful home."

Justice shook Dominica's hand and said, "Nice to meet you too."

Poose ran into the living room. Jordan jumped up on Justice's sectional, "Ah shit!" She screamed.

Poose tried to jump on her as Jordan kicked at her, "Poose! No! Get down! Sit!" Justice screamed.

"Yeah! Please get Kujo out of here," Jordan requested.

Justice grabbed Poose by the collar dragging her into the other room. Jordan slowly climbed down from the sectional making sure Poose was gone. Justice returned to the living room.

"My bad girl for jumping on your furniture, but I didn't know you had an animal. You need to tell people in advance you got protectors," Jordan apologized.

"I'm sorry. I didn't know you were afraid of dogs."

"Afraid?…No! I don't like," Jordan replied.

"Y'all want a drink or what?" Justice asked.

"No thank you. I'll drink plenty when I get there," Dominica said with a heavy Hispanic accent.

"I'll take one. Dark not light," Jordan requested.

Justice walked into the kitchen. She grabbed a chilled glass out of the mini refrigerator behind the bar. She grabbed the crystal jar filled with Brandy and poured Jordan a shot. She brought the glass out to Jordan handing it to her. "Thank you much," Jordan said. She inhaled it all in one quick swallow. She rubbed her chest because it burned, "Mm! This some good shit! I got chest hairs now." She handed the glass back to Justice. Justice placed the glass on the cocktail table. She grabbed her purse off of the sectional.

"You ready for a wild night?" Jordan asked.

"I'm down for anything about now," Justice admitted.

"That's all I need to hear. Let's go," Jordan replied.

They all exited Justice's condo.

***

On the ride to the mysterious club, Justice sat in the backseat of Jordan's Durango staring out of the window. Jordan blasted the music as her and Dominica talked and laughed. Justice giggled to herself in response to her employee's actions. Jordan seemed like a fun person. Justice wondered why she waited so long to hang out with her.

After 45 minutes of riding, they finally pulled up in the club's parking lot. Justice read the title of the club aloud, "Erotic Characteristics? Sounds like the title of a strip club."

"Oh! You haven't seen anything like this," Dominica responded.

"Jordan, please don't tell me, knowing how horny I am, that you have taken me to a strip club to be teased," Justice stated.

"Teased? No! Trust me. Tonight you're getting a fix for that 4 years itch. Trust me. You will become a regular here," Jordan enlightened.

"I guess. I'm ready to see what this is about," Justice said.

"Grab your things ladies. Time to have the time of our lives," Jordan said as she opened the door.

They all got out then the valet attendant climbed in and parked the truck. Justice viewed the scenery as they entered the club. The first thing she noticed was the palm trees; four of them in large marble in appearance plant pots – three feet in diameter. Justice thought to herself, *Where in the hell did they get palm trees? This is the Midwest.* She noticed the two stretch, Cadillac Escalade limousines parked curbside; one pearl and the other black. Lights lined the outer corners of the club as the red carpet was laid out like a movie premiere. She was impressed so far.

While standing at the entrance, Justice noticed a light-skinned man inside of the club. He caught her attention immediately. He was around 6'0", athletic built, with the short tapered curly Afro. Chills shot down her spin as she peered at him. He disappeared into the crowd.

Dominica and Jordan already paid their entrance fee now it was Justice's turn. "That'll be $100," Miley said.

"What? How much?" Justice questioned.

"General admission is $100."

"$100?" Justice blurted.

"Just pay it Justice. Trust me, it's worth it," Jordan said.

"I have never paid more than $25 to get in a club. This is some bullshit; legalized robbery."

Justice reached into her purse and pulled out $300. She counted out $100 in $20 bills. She handed the money to Miley shoving the difference back into her purse. "Have a great time," Miley said.

"I better!" Justice stated with attitude.

***

They found a table and sat down. They sat near the stage with Justice sitting across from the stage facing the stage. There was a man on stage stripping, but Justice wasn't paying him much attention. She observed the club. On the opposite end of the club, they had women stripping. There were small rooms surrounding the club. She noticed people going in and out of those rooms. There were three bars, a food kitchen where they served all kinds of food from chicken wings to enchiladas, pool tables sprinkled throughout, and big screen T.V.'s along the walls. Porno's played on most of the televisions while a few showed sports, increasing Justice's arousal.

"I'm a get us some drinks," Jordan said as she walked off.

Ten minutes passed and she returned with a tray full of drinks. She happily passed them out. Justice had two shots of Brandy and a jello shot in front of her. Jordan had two double shots of 151, and Dominica had two Amaretto Sours. Justice quickly downed her drinks and inhaled her jello shot.

A half an hour passed and they were feeling their drinks. All of them were laughing and giggling.

"Whatever! I don't care girl," Jordan said while laughing.

"You're just a freak. You nasty bitch," Dominica blurted while laughing so hard she could barely speak.

"You didn't say that last night, now did you?" Jordan responded.

Justice was shocked, "You mean…"

Jordan smiled, "Yes. Dominica is my bitch."

Dominica stared at Jordan and said, "I thought you were my bitch."

"Nope. Sorry. You're my bitch," Jordan stated.

As Jordan and Dominica debated, Justice noticed the man she saw when she first walked in. He sat at a table by himself drinking a beer. She stared as his lips gently touching the bottle. She watched as he took a swig. She examined him up and down. He had on a black tight fitting t-shirt hugging his physique. He had on a pair of dark denim jeans and some black casual shoes. He had his left ear pierced with a small diamond stud. He had long thin sideburns that flowed down into his closely shaved goatee. Jordan turned her head to see what had Justice's full, undivided attention, "You want him?" Jordan said.

"Nah! He fine though," Justice admitted as she peered over at him again.

"Girl you better go over there, take him to a room, and handle yours," Dominica said.

"What?"

"He's clean. Everybody here has a clean bill of health," Dominica added.

"What do you mean?"

"This is a swinger's club Justice. We come here to fuck," Jordan said then laughed.

"So those rooms are for…"

"Fucking. Yes!" Jordan admitted.

Justice sat quiet for a few seconds.

"Don't worry Justice. Nobody will know. Also, you won't catch anything. The men are on papers. They're clean. They have to have a clean bill of health to work here, and they're checked regularly," Dominica enlightened.

"Lighten up boss. We come here all the time. It's cool. Now if you'll excuse us, we have some business to attend to. You ready Dominica?" Jordan said.

While standing, Dominica said, "Yes! Let's go!" Dominica and Jordan both got up from the table.

"Loosen up. You'll be fine," Dominica advised. They walked away disappearing into the crowd.

Justice sat quietly as she thought: *I know I'm horny, but damn. I'm not desperate. This is wild. I've never been to a swinger's club before. I'm not sure if I'm down with this. I've never had sex with someone I don't know before. I don't know how many women these men have had. I'm cool. I'll just drink my drink, tip some strippers, and call it a night.*

"Excuse me," A deep voice with a heavy Jamaican accent said.

Justice turned around. She stared into the face of the man she had been staring at all night.

"Is anyone sitting here?" He said.

"No! Not at all."

"May I sit with you?" He asked.

"Sure."

He sat down next to Justice. Justice was so nervous her heart raced and hands trembled a little. He smelled so good. His smell turned her on double time almost like a love potion.

"I'm Marlo," he said while extending his hand for Justice to shake.

While shaking his hand, "I'm Justice."

"Nice to meet you Justice. What brings you out tonight?" he questioned.

"Some friends of mine brought me here to get me out of the house."

"Same here. My brother wanted me to 'chill out'. I'm a Rheumatologist. I work 14 sometimes 18 hours a day at the children's hospital. I really don't have time to meet people."

"Same here. I work my life away. I really don't have time to meet people either, so I know how you feel." Justice confessed.

"What do you do for a living?"

"I'm a small business owner," Justice said.

"Interesting. I've always wanted my own practice. That's very commendable," he stated while staring Justice up and down.

"Thank you. Waiter!" Justice screamed for the waiter.

The waiter walked towards them carrying her empty serving tray in the palm of her hand, "Yes!"

"A shot of Greygoose," Justice requested.

"And you Sir?" The waiter asked.

"Beer. Any kind."

The waiter walked away.

"Do you have any children?" Marlo questioned.

"No! Not ready for that yet. Do you have any?"

"Unfortunately no. I want a family, but with my schedule, it's almost impossible."

"I understand that. So when you do have a family, what do you want? Girls? Boys? A mixture?" Justice enquired.

"It really doesn't matter as long as they are healthy."

"Well, how many do you want?"

"About two maybe three. You?" Marlo questioned.

"I only want one, a girl."

The waiter returned with the drinks, "That will be $6.50 for yours (Justice) and $3.75 for yours (Marlo)."

Justice reached into her purse. Marlo gently grabbed her hand stopping her, "I got it."

Justice nodded her head silently saying, "Okay".

Marlo paid the waiter then he took a swig of his beer.

"So, what are you here for?" Justice asked.

"For you."

"Excuse me?"

"I'm not going to beat around the bush. You are beautiful. You are gorgeous. You are the classiest woman in here. You're bad! I saw you when you first walked in and wondered all night how to approach you. I almost didn't come over here," Marlo explained.

"Wow! Thank you for the complement."

"Look, I don't usually do this. I don't usually come to places like this. I know after I say this you might slap me in my face, but I have to be honest," Marlo nervously stated.

"Say what?" Justice questioned.

"I really want to taste you. I want to fuck you," Marlo said then smiled in embarrassment.

Justice paused to soak in what Marlo just said to her. She inhaled her drink. She sat quietly for a couple of seconds staring into space.

"I apologize if I offended you. You have a good evening Mrs. Justice," Marlo quickly apologized, grabbed his beer then stood.

Justice grabbed a hold of his forearm, "You should wait until you get cursed out or hear 'no' before you exit."

"What?"

"I don't recall saying, 'no,'" Justice said as she smiled.

Marlo stuck his hand out for Justice to grab. Justice grabbed his hand and stood up.

"I've never done this before," she admitted.

"Neither have I. Don't worry. I will call you in the morning," he smiled.

"You better," Justice walked away with him.

***

As soon as they entered into the private room, they both kissed each other passionately. Marlo grabbed Justice by the bottom of her ass picking her up. He put her against the wall pressing his fully erect penis against her. Justice's pussy throbbed. She had been yearning for something similar to this for four years. Marlo kissed her on her neck deeply, intensely, and roughly- even bit her a few times. Chills ran throughout her body as she obliged the erotic sensation. She embraced him; rubbing his head like she was rubbing a ball while he continued sucking on her neck. His lips smoothly massaged the tension off of her. She was so turned on her juices flowed like a raging river headed downstream dampening the lining of her panties.

Marlo gently laid Justice on the twin bed in the room. He took his shirt off revealing a chiseled body with abs that rippled like a valley full of mountains as he tossed his shirt onto the floor. Justice rubbed her hands up and down his chiseled abs. His skin was as soft as a woman's. Marlo stared Justice in her eyes with an expression that silently said, "I want you so bad it hurts". He tenderly rubbed the backside of his hand up and down Justice's inner thigh, "It's okay if you change your mind. We don't have to do this if you don't want to."

"The fuck we don't! You started this. If you stop now, I'm a have to cut you. You better fuck the shit out of me," Justice stated.

"I never stop," Marlo said as he smoothly slid her heels off and unbuttoned her pants. With one swift pull, he snatched both her panties and her pants off simultaneously gently throwing them onto the floor. Justice was so aroused she eagerly ripped her own shirt and bra from her body.

Justice lied on the bed facing him slightly leaning up. She used her elbows to keep her back lightly lifted off the mattress. Her body yearned for a taste of this beautiful man as she stared at Marlo with her piercing bedroom eyes. Marlo unzipped his pants stepping out of them holding them in his hand. His dick showed definition underneath his boxers. He was very well endowed as he slid his boxers off and Justice admired his naked physique. He reached into his pants pocket, pulled out a condom, tossed his pants to the floor, opened the condom, and slid it on.

Marlo slowly climbed on top of Justice. He massaged her neck with his lips again. She massaged his back with her hands welcoming the feeling. He moved up to her lips as they kissed passionately for a few seconds. Marlo went over and nibbled on her right ear. Justice squired as she ug her nails into his back. Marlo's body waved in response silently telling her he liked to be scratched. Justice dug her nails into his back again as he bit down on her neck at the crease where the neck and shoulder connect. Justice clinched her legs around his waist. Marlo moved down to her nipples blowing on one while thumbing the other. He gently wrapped his lips around her nipple and moved the tip of his tongue around in slow circular motions. Justice dug her nails into his back yet again and whispered, "Shit." Marlo went to the other nipple and repeated. Justice grabbed his head and made him kiss her. They kissed passionately again as Justice embraced him rubbing her hands all across his back. Marlo whispered in her ear with that strong Jamaican accent, "I want to taste you." He licked a trail from her neck down to the top of her pubic hair. He gently blew across her pubic hair and her panty line. It felt so good Justice allowed a small moan to escape her lips. Marlo placed her legs over his shoulders. He licked and kissed Justice's inner thighs with those soft, full lips as she bit down on her bottom lip trying to prevent another moan from escaping.

Marlo licked in between her vaginal lips. Justice squirmed obliging the feeling. He continued to slowly lick up and down her lips before nibbling on them. He spread her lips wide open with his index and middle fingers revealing a fully erect clitoris. He licked the clitoris up and down with the tip of his tongue swiftly mimicking the motion of a butterfly's wings fluttering.

Justice arced her back breathing intensely trying her hardest not to scream or moan the pleasure. With her legs still over his shoulders, Marlo climbed on top of Justice. As he climbed upon her, he injected his dick into her slobbering wet pussy. Justice whispered, "Ah yeah." Her knees touched her shoulders as he thrust deep and slow. The pleasure was so intense that Justice wanted to run away from him, but he had her locked in one place, one position. "Shit! Shit! Ah!" was all Justice could say as he entered in and out of her forcefully. The feeling was so good that she soon became absolutely speechless. All she could do at this point was dig her nails into his back. He continued injecting her deep and fast. Her legs trembled as her waste jerked. She had the most forceful, longest lasting orgasm of her life.

They continued fucking until neither one of them could take it anymore…and yes…he called her in the morning.

Tangeray

Introduction

I lied on my side leaning against my arm with the palm of my hand resting underneath my chin. My hair pulled into a jet-black silky ponytail that stopped in the middle of my back. My thin one-inch thick gold crown decorated my head as my black shear teddy hugged my body perfectly revealing my assets. My eyes were smoky yet colorful; Egyptianized – Cleopatra would be envious.

Two husky men wearing nothing more than bikini styled underwear exhibiting the tools they were working with carried me into the room as though I was a delicate desert. One in front of me, the other behind me, as I lied sexily on the red chastise they held firmly within their grasp. Examining my surroundings with my eyes, I noticed a double king-sized canopy styled bed accented and trimmed in 24 ct gold. Red satiny looking sheets covered the mattress as mountains of pillows kept the head board company.

The men stopped at the foot of the bed slowly lowering my black suede chastise. Once the chastise touched the shiny marble floor, each man held out his strong hand standing on each side of me as I sat up locking hands with theirs. They gently pulled me to a standing position as my sandals kissed the floor, and I was lifted up by my forearms and laid gently onto the bed. I scooted towards the middle of the bed swimming on top of the satin sheets feeling them tickle my medium brown skin as I lied on my side in a loose fetal-type position.

One of the men grabbed a golden tray and sat it next to the bed on its stand. He grabbed some oil and climbed onto the bed as the dim candlelight gave his golden complexion a diffused glow with shadows adding definition to his already chiseled physique. With every movement, his muscles flexed as he stared intently at my thick pear-shaped frame admiring my tank ass as the teddy rose up revealing my flesh.

Once he was as close as arms length away from me, he poured some oil into the palm of his hands, grabbed my foot, massaged the oil into the sole, between my perfectly manicured toes, and on top of my foot all the way up to my calf; rubbing in small circular motions –went down and repeated on the other foot. The other man climbed onto the bed looking like a pit-bull, slowly on his hands and knees. I turned onto my back arching it a bit staring at him with my vision upside down. He crawled towards me hovering as he softly kissed my lips; his bottom on my top and my top on his bottom.

I stared into his blue eyes; had never seen a black man with blue eyes before and they could be seen even within the dimness of the hue from the candlelight – sparkling like a gemstone. I leaned up; just had to have another one of those kisses. He kissed me again – his full lips shaped like a cupid's bow. As we kissed, I felt the other man rub his hands up the inside of my thighs from my knees to my panty line as the blue-eyed man grabbed my wrists, stretching my arms out above my head, and pinning them to the bed.

I stared down at the man between my legs staring into his lustful eyes; low, dark-brown, and sensual. He opened his mouth and bit down on my pussy licking my clit upwards as he closed his mouth sucking my juices. I squirmed, breathed hard, as I tilted my head back biting my bottom lip. He repeated as the other man leaned up sucking on my neck with his lips and tongue. I moaned as I closed my eyes.

I heard someone beating on the door downstairs. I opened my eyes and the two men had vanished; the double king-sized bed, the large suite in the palace were gone within a blink – I sighed. It was just a dream; a damn good one at that…damnit!…

My Man's Friend

It's early in the morning on a hot, humid summer day. I awakened to someone banging on my door. "Damn! Who is this?" I said to myself aloud. I climbed out of my bed and walked downstairs in an irritated fashion hoping the banging noise wouldn't wake up my kids.

I approached the door with a mass attitude. First, I didn't like being woke up. Second, it's 10 O'clock in the morning, and it's already 85 degrees. I didn't have any air conditioning, and I'm slightly hung over.

I opened the door, and to my surprise, there were two police officers standing here. "Can I help you?" I asked.

"Yeah, we have a warrant for Mr. Stewart. Is he here?" one of the officers responded loudly.

"No! He's not. What is this about?" I questioned sternly.

"He would have to tell you that," the other officer stated.

"Well, he's not here," After I said that, I heard my baby crying.

"Okay ma'am. If you see him, let him know that we have a warrant for him."

"Alright," I responded then I slammed the door shut.

Fuck! Loud ass police done woke up my baby. Those fucking bastards! Ain't this about a bitch? I had one more hour of peace until they showed the fuck up. To add, while pointing at my boyfriend's picture, this sorry ass nigga was about to go to prison again. No good for nothing loser. What was I thinking getting with him? What was I thinking having kids with him? What was I thinking?

***

I ran upstairs to my baby's room. My two year old was in here trying to calm his little sister down. He was climbing into the crib. I grabbed a hold of him, "Get down. You can hurt yourself." I stood him on the floor. I'm pissed all over again. Jamaal wet his pants again. He looked at me and said, "I'm big boy. I'm big boy."

As I grabbed my baby girl out of the crib, I said, "You are a big boy Jamaal. You're just not big enough to climb inside of Sasha's bed, okay?"

"Okay," Jamaal replied with his head tilted down.

"Let's get you some dry underwear," I mumbled as we walked into his bedroom.

***

I put some clean underwear on Jamaal then I took the kids downstairs. I sat Jamaal in his high chair. I sat Sasha in her walker. I made Jamaal some Cream of Wheat, and I gave Sasha some baby cereal. While feeding Sasha her cereal, I heard another knock at the door. "Damn! Who is it now?" I said to myself aloud.

I got up and opened the door. It's Rome my boyfriend Jasper's friend, "Hi you doing Tangeray?" Rome blurted with a big smile on his face.

"Shit! Pissed!" I admitted.

"Damn! Sorry to hear that baby girl. Jaz here?" Rome questioned.

"Nah!" I replied with my hand on my hip.

"You mind if I wait for him? He told me to meet him over here," he requested.

"Nah! I don't mind," I let him in.

Rome walked towards Sasha. While picking her up, he said, "Hey pretty girl. You getting so big looking just like your momma."

Sasha cooed at him smiling. She grabbed his face trying to kiss him. She must be thinking the same thing I'm thinking, *Damn, he is fine.*

As I sat across from Rome, I felt as nervous as a criminal walking down the green mile. Rome was so fine. He's the type of fine that made your pussy throb every single time you looked at him. He was 6'2", dark smooth chocolate complexion, body like 50 cent's, and he had light brown eyes. I had never seen a dark-skinned man with light eyes before. He had smooth, big soft looking lips, and dimples so deep I could see them when he spoke. On top of that, he had on a tank top and had tattoos all over his strong muscular arms. He had a clean-cut haircut, and he was bow-legged with track runner's legs. Mmm! All I can say was, *I sho' wouldn't mind.*

Rome sat on the couch playing with Sasha. I picked Jamaal up out of the high chair and brought him into the living room. Rome stared at me as I returned. I nervously said, "What?"

Jamaal ran over to Rome jumping on him, "Hey Wome."

Rome smiled as he tickled Jamaal, "What's been good Maal?"

"Nothing," Jamaal said while giggling.

"My bad. I'm not trying to ignore you," Rome said.

I walked to the chair and sat down, "I was just wondering why you was looking."

Rome smiled as he licked his lips. *Damn don't do that,* I said to myself. He said, "Nah! I was looking at your hair. It's different. I like it."

"I'm surprised you noticed," I expressed with attitude.

"What? I notice everything about you. You not used to complements or something?"

"No!" I confessed.

"You telling me Jaz never complement you?"

"That nigga don't notice shit," I blurted.

"Niggah's boy! Ain't no damn way. If I had a woman like…He dumb as fuck. That's all I can say," Rome replied while turning his head away from me.

"What else were you going to say?" I asked.

"Nothing. Nothing at all," Rome quickly said.

We both sat here quiet for a few seconds. Suddenly, Jasper walked in through the back door as loud as usual. "I'm home!" he screamed.

I just sat here wishing he would go back to wherever he came from. He strode into the living room. "Romy, Rome! What up boy?" He shook his hand.

"Shit. What's good?" Rome said.

"I'll get to that in a second," Jasper said then continued, "Where's breakfast?"

"Waiting for you to cook it," I replied.

"See, This the type of shit I'm talking about. A man can't get a little breakfast? Damn! It's bad enough you not giving me any pussy. Can I at least get a hot meal?" Jasper said in an irritated fashion.

"Can you at least get a fucking job? Maybe if you lasted more than 2 minutes I would give you some pussy."

"Fuck you!" Jasper yelled.

"If you knew how, I might let you. By the way, the police came by here. You got a warrant play boy."

"Shit! When did they come?"

"About 30 minutes ago. You better be careful. They might be sitting outside watching the house. What you do this time?" I questioned.

"Don't worry about that."

"What you mean, don't worry about that? Ain't you tired of going in and out of there?" I screamed.

"Yeah, but what else am I supposed to do?"

"Stop committing crimes! Damn! How hard is that?"

"You don't get it. I'm trying to get paper. Don't start with me today," Jasper said as he walked away from me.

"Don't start. Don't start!" I screamed.

"We got company damn! Don't be ignorant."

"I hate you!" I screamed.

"Rome, let me handle this. I'll get at you in a second. Sit tight."

Rome said, "Alright."

Jasper grabbed my arm pulling me to the side, "Let me talk to you upstairs."

I was so irritated, "I don't want to talk to you. I'm tired Jasper. I am so tired and fed up. There's nothing to discuss anymore."

"Please! We need to talk," Jasper said in a mellow 'I apologize' tone.

I stared at him with evil eyes for a couple of seconds. Then I walked upstairs as Jasper followed me.

I walked into my bedroom. Jasper walked in and shut the door. He walked up behind me and hugged me from behind. He put his hands on my breasts and rubbed his dick against my ass. "Tang, you know I love you right?" He whispered.

"No, I don't. If you love me, why won't you help me?"

"What you talking about? I do help you?" He replied.

"With what? You're never here. You pay a bill every blue moon. You're demanding," I shook my head in disapproval.

"I'm sorry. I been stressed. I been looking for jobs, but you know how it is. Nobody is going to hire me with two felonies babe. You can hate me all day, but I'm fucking trying. I made a big move last night. I hit a big ass lick. I know you tired of me going in and out, but I swere this is the last time. The boom I hit will have us straight for a very long time."

While removing his hands from my body and turning to face him, I said, "I'm tired of this shit Jaz. I'm tired of living like this. I'm twenty three with four kids. I don't have a fucking life. I'm tired of living in this piece of shit apartment and being in this damn neighborhood. I want better. I deserve better. I'm tired of you cheating, and I'm tired of you going in and out of prison. If I'm doing this by myself, I my-as-well be by myself."

"So you leaving me?"

"I don't know. I don't know. I'm just fed up. I don't know how much more I can take."

"I promise I haven't messed with anyone else after the last one. I am better now. There's enough money now for you to move the kids out of here. There's enough for you to go to nursing school. You always wanted to be a nurse. Now you can. I'm trying the best I know how. Trust me. It'll get better," Jasper begged.

"So what now? How long you gonna be gone this time?" I asked.

"Not too long okay. Trust me," Jasper said then gave me a passionate kiss.

I really didn't want him touching me right now. I believed that I had fallen out of love with him. Back in the day, I was happy to see him. I used to be pissed whenever I couldn't be around him. Now, I didn't even miss him when he's gone. I was irritated every time he walked through the door.

Jasper had done so much to me. He had cheated on me so many times I lost count two years ago. He had an outside kid the same age as each one of our kids and one on the way. He always says that this is the last time. He said that when he got his first outside kid. Not to mention, I couldn't count on him for nothing. He didn't pay any bills; he didn't do anything for our kids, and he's always in and out of prison or jail. Then when it came to lovemaking, he's only pleased me a handful of times. Most of the time, he's in it for himself. He beats it up and two minutes later he's done. I didn't even know why I was letting him do this.

I was on the bed stomach down with my butt in the air. Jasper stood behind me rubbing his dick up and down my pussy. "Oooh…I'm 'bout to tear this up," Jasper said. I rolled my eyes wishing he would rush and get this over with.

Jasper jammed his dick in my pussy. "Mmm!" I said. I couldn't believe that actually felt good. *Was it a cold day in hell?* I thought as Jasper penetrated forcefully yet slow. Okay, I'm liking this. I might actually get something out of this. He continued to inject slow and hard. Ooh! This felt so damn good. Keep it coming. Keep it coming. Jasper started injecting deep and fast. It felt good, but I know him. I knew what this meant. Two minutes later he pulled out nutting on my back. I hated when he did that.

"Why'd you have to do that?" I asked.

"Do what?"

While getting up, "Get it off my back," I sternly said.

Jasper grabbed a towel from the closet and wiped the nut off of my back. "My bad," he said with a smile on his face.

I climbed down from the bed. I bent down grabbing my underwear. Jasper stood in front of me with his dick out. "Suck my dick," he demanded.

I stared at him in dismay.

"You gone suck my dick?" He asked in a whiny tone.

"No!"

"Why not?" He questioned.

"Because you don't…fuck it!" I got down on my knees and put his dick in my mouth. Normally, I would start slow then give him the works. Instead, I simply went for it; sucking hard and fast. I wanted him to come quickly as usual, but I'm also trying to bruise him so he won't ask anymore.

Just as I expected, he nutted within another two minutes; he pulled his pants up and again he's out the door. I stood here in silence. If this was making love, I wonder what it's like to fuck. I wondered what it would be like to fuck Rome. I was horny as fuck now. I wondered if Rome would let me. I knew it's wrong to think sexual thoughts about my man's best friend. However, I didn't know how much longer I could go with being left aroused like this. Masturbating purely wasn't hitting the spot.

***

A half an hour passed and my kids were asleep. I loved the fact that they took early naps. I walked upstairs and turned the shower on. I took my clothes off and climbed in. I stood in this hot shower horny as hell. The warm water splattered across my breasts. I turned around to allow the water to massage my back. I rubbed my shoulders gently with my hands crossed in front of me. I stared at the wall deep in thought. I pictured Rome standing in front of me in the shower. I could see the water dripping down his chiseled chest. I imagined rubbing his chest with my hands and licking the water off with my tongue. I visualized me putting my hand around his large chocolate dick. "Ahh! Fuck!" I screamed as I backed away from the showerhead. The water got ice cold on me. Nothing except cold water sprayed from the spout. I jumped out of the shower in a hurry to get away from the frigid water. I couldn't stand this piece of shit apartment.

I was in my room getting dressed. I examined myself in the mirror. I looked damn good to have four kids. I didn't have one stretch mark or blemish on my body. I was in great shape. My stomach was flat, and I'm getting my six-pack back. I didn't look like I had a baby 8 months ago.

I wanted so badly to dump Jasper and find me a new man. I knew I could do better than him. Honestly, I felt stuck. It's almost impossible for me to move on. I had four kids. What young man wanted to get with a woman who has four kids already? I didn't want to be alone, but I wasn't satisfied here. I'm not happy here. I guess what Tyvid said was true. I'm bored with him now. He's predictable now. The bad boy has lost his thrill.

***

Twenty more minutes passed, and my mother was here. I was in my room putting the finishing touches on my hair. I sprayed on some perfume. I stared in the mirror. Not to sound conceited, but I looked damn good. I wore a white tank top, some hip-hugging capri's, and a pair of open toe heels, *gone girl.*

I walked downstairs, and my mother sat on the couch holding Sasha in her arms. "Hey Momma!" I said.

"Hey baby. You look cute."

"Thank you."

"What did you do to your hair?" she asked.

"I styled it," I responded.

"Why you always putting that weave in your hair? You got long hair of your own. See, in the 70's we were natural. If it ain't natural, it ain't right. What's wrong with you young girls? Are you ashamed of yourselves?" Momma questioned.

"No! What makes you say that?" I asked while sitting down in the chair.

"Perming your hair and weaving your hair. Black is beautiful. Wear the hair God gave you and get some air up in here. These babies look like little wet noodles. Shit, I'm a lose twenty pounds sitting up in here. If I had high blood pressure, I'd have a damn stroke."

"I can't afford an air conditioner," I admitted.

"What about that man you got up in here. Make him buy one."

"Yeah right," I said.

"Baby, if he ain't helping you, then you don't need him. Nothing on this earth is free except for the air we breathe and pretty soon we'll be paying for that shit."

I collected Jamaal and Sasha's bags. I handed them to momma. While putting the bags across her shoulder, "Where Shyeesha and Jasper Jr.?" momma asked.

"Tyman got them this weekend."

While getting up from the couch, "Okay."

Momma walked to the door holding Sasha. I gave Jamaal a big hug and a kiss. I grabbed his hand and walked him to momma's car.

I sat Jamaal in his car seat while momma put Sasha in hers. I snapped him in, gave him a hug. He said, "Later momma." I winked at him and blew him a kiss then walked to the other side of the car to give Sasha a soft kiss goodbye.

"You have some fun now. Not too much fun though. I don't want any more of these popping out of you," Momma added.

"I'm not having any more kids momma."

"That's what you said when Shyeesha was born. Be smart. Get them tubes tied, you hear?" Momma said while getting into the car.

"Yeah! Bye!" I sarcastically blurted as I returned to the house.

***

Hours had passed. Thank God my mother came and got the two kids I had here. My oldest kids, Shyeesha (7 years old) and Jasper Jr. (4 years old), were with my younger sister for the weekend. I lain across my couch in front of the fan watching television. This ain't helping at all. This fan blew hot air around the entire apartment. I'm bored, and I'm still horny. I was so fucking irritated.

I heard a knock at the door. I was so drained from the humidity I really don't feel like getting up. I screamed, "Come in."

The neighbor's son walked in, "Mrs. Tangeray, momma said you got some sugar?"

"Yeah, you know where it is," I mumbled.

Little Tywain walked into the kitchen and got some sugar. "Thanks," he said.

"Don't forget to bring my container back," I reminded.

"Okay. I will", he said as he walked out of the door.

Only in the projects I tell you. These neighbors borrow everything from sugar to your blow dryer. It tripped me out when the little girl down the alley came over to borrow my iron. I barely even knew her mother, and she asked for my iron? I got to get up out of here. Although I was raised here, I couldn't continue living like this. I wanted more. I needed more.

I got off the couch and walked to my kitchen. As soon as I turned the kitchen light on, roaches scattered. This was too fucking much. I grabbed the bottle of Absolute from the counter. I poured half of a 12 oz glass. I opened the refrigerator and poured orange juice into the other half of the glass. I returned to the couch. I grabbed the stereo remote from my coffee table. I turned some slow jams on and dove into my drink. I showed no mercy as I downed the entire glass in less than two minutes. Before I knew it, I was feeling it. I'm not drunk, but got one hell of a buzz.

I sang and danced by myself having a one-person party. Suddenly, the phone rang. I picked it up. "Hello!" I screamed over the music.

"You have a collect call from an inmate in Barzen County jail. To take this call there is a $2.50 charge. Do you accept this charge?" The automated system said.

"Yes!" I screamed as I turned the music down.

"Your call is being connected."

"Tang, this your man. Call Rome. He got something for you," Jasper blurted.

"I don't have his number."

"555-1680."

"So how much time you got now?" I questioned.

"Don't know until I go to court. My lawyer trying to get me a plea of 18 months," He explained.

"18 months! Okay," I hung the phone up, "Fuck him!" I screamed aloud. The phone rang again. I ignored and let it ring.

After five minutes of letting the phone ring back to back, I finally called Rome. The phone rang twice. "Yep!" Rome said.

"Rome, this is Tang. Jaz told me to call you."

"Yeah, I'll be over there in about a half. Is that okay?" He asked.

"Yeah. That's fine. Just come on in. You don't have to knock."

"Alright. See you then."

I hung the phone up and screamed. Rome was coming over, and I was totally alone. I planned to make my move. Normally, I would feel bad for even the thought of doing something like this. However, with all Jasper had done to me, I was well within my right. Why should I remain the innocent party? A wrong and a right don't make a right. The old adage is two wrongs don't make a right. Well, according to the laws of integers, two negatives do in fact equal a positive; Hello! If Rome obliged, there would be a positive outcome, revenge, and a good ass feeling. I know he can fuck. I could tell by his demeanor. His essence screamed, "I'll fuck the shit out of any woman, including you, you, and you."

I was so excited I didn't know what to do. I ran upstairs and stood in front of the mirror. I examined myself. I looked nice. I looked good. What's missing from my attire?…Make-up. I ran to my dresser mirror and pulled out my make-up case. I carefully and skillfully applied my make-up. Now, I resembled a model. I looked good enough to be on the cover of a magazine.

***

Downstairs, I fixed me another cocktail. I slowly drank it. Afterwards, I smoked a cigarette to heighten my buzz. I put a slow mix CD in my bookcase stereo system that rested on my entertainment stand. I played the music loudly, but low enough to hear myself speak. I stretched out across the couch lying on my back. I put my hands above my head fluttering my fingers across the arm.

Rome walked in. I turned my head towards him. He stood here wearing a white tank top, some baggy denim shorts, footies, and some flip-flops. He had a one inch thick white gold herringbone necklace around his neck and a 2ct diamond earring in his left ear. He had a small black duffle bag in his hand.

I leaned up staring at him. He smiled. I sat up to allow him to sit on the couch next to me. "I see you. You in here jamming. I take it the kids must be gone," Rome said as he sat next to me on the couch.

"Yes they are. I am so happy. I love my babies, but I need a break," I admitted.

While peaking in my glass, he said, "What you drinking on momma?"

"Absolute and cranberry."

"That's my shit,"

"You want one? I can make you a drink," I offered.

"Nah! I'm good. Thanks anyway," Rome said as he glanced around the living room.

Me and Rome sat here for a hot second in silence. I slyly stared at Rome. He appeared a little nervous. I rubbed his shoulder and said, "What's wrong?"

He stared at me then turned away, "Nothing…Jaz got knocked."

"I know. He called."

"He wanted me to give you this," Rome handed me the duffle bag.

I grabbed the duffle bag and opened it up. It was full of money. "What the fuck?" I shouted.

"Tell me about it!"

"How much is this?"

"I don't know. Jaz want you to have it though. He said buy a house for you and the kids and go to school," Rome stated.

I was happy yet surprised. Jaz actually came through for us. I felt like I woke up in the Twilight Zone. I pinched myself. This was actually real. It looked like it was about $250,000 in this bag.

Rome laid the duffle bag on the floor and stood. I stood and asked, "Where are you going?"

"I figure you might want to go out and spend some of that."

"I do, but it doesn't feel right."

"What do you mean?"

"Aren't you tired? We're better than this gutter living."

Rome paused, "Hey, Jaz is just my friend. I don't do what he do. I work hard. I pay taxes."

"Why don't you stay a while…keep me company?"

Rome stood silent. He cut his eyes in the opposite direction trying not to look at me. I stood close in front of him violating his intimate space. I gently grabbed his face to make him look me in my eyes. Rome stared into my eyes.

"I want you to fuck me."

"What?...I mean you fine, but you're Jaz's girl…I don't roll like that," Rome explained.

"Fuck Jaz!" I walked away from Rome then turned facing him, "Look at my life. I've been with this clown since ninth grade. I don't even know why. I'm not sure if I love him anymore or if I want to be with him. All I know is…I want you. Just one moment; I want you. Nobody will know but us…I promise."

"I don't know Tang."

I went to him violating his intimate space yet again, "Fuck me Rome. Fuck me please."

"I…I would, but…"

I grabbed Rome's face giving him a very passionate, lustful kiss. While kissing me, Rome gently rubbed up and down the small of my back. His touch brought chills down my spine as every single body hair on me stood erect. I couldn't believe Rome was actually kissing me in return. I pressed up against him. My pussy throbbed because I could feel his manhood. I knew he had a big dick.

Rome suddenly pulled away from the kiss as he took a step back.

"Don't stop. Please don't stop," I begged.

"I'm not. I want to look at you," Rome carefully examined my body with his eyes. He stared at me like he could see through my clothes. The way he looked at me turned me on tremendously. I stood frozen as my panties moistened. "One moment," he said. He walked to the front door, closing it then locking it.

I walked to the stereo and turned the volume up. Rome grabbed the duffle bag full of money. We stared at each other eye to eye for a couple of seconds. We both communicated with our thoughts because we both wanted this bad as hell. I walked towards Rome. I gently grabbed his hand. "Come on," I calmly stated trying to sound extremely sexy. I lured Rome upstairs into my bedroom.

***

The sun was setting as the hue in my room was dim but not dark. The stereo was up so loud that we both could hear it, as though, it was in this room with us. As soon as we walked in the room, we both kissed passionately. By the way he kissed me, I could tell that this was something he's been waiting to do for quite some time now. We walked towards my bed while kissing and stroking one another.

I lied on the bed on my back. Rome hovered over me at the edge of the bed. He unzipped the duffle bag dumping the money all over the bed. He removed his tank top tossing it on the floor. I was in awe staring at him. He had sweat dripping down the middle of his chest from his neck. His forehead beaded with sweat because of the humidity of this apartment and the rising of his body temperature. He slowly climbed on top of me like a bow legged pit-bull on all fours. He rubbed his hands up my legs. The hairs on my legs stood up as a tickling feeling flowed up to my pussy. I throbbed and slowly pulsated. He breathed up the inner lining of my capri's until his face was in between my legs. He gently nibbled for about 10 seconds breathing hard onto it. I squirmed in response. He ripped my capri's off while kissing and licking my inner thigh following the skin trail the capri's revealed as he yanked them off. He threw them across the room. He climbed back on top breathing on my pussy as I grabbed his head to welcome the good mood. He gently licked my panty line making me want to climb the walls. He carefully removed my panties rubbing the inside of my lips with his fingers. "Damn!" I softly whispered. He gave a subtle smirk revealing them gorgeous ass dimples.

He breathed on my pussy then licked up and down each lip. While he licked my lips, he injected his fingers in me finger fucking me. He began slow and deep pulling it out and gently sliding it back in. The entire time he was finger fucking me, he stared into my eyes and gently bit down on his bottom lip. I reached down putting my hands in his pants. I held his dick as I stroked it trying to give him the same pleasure he gave me. Suddenly, he switched up on me. He slid his fingers in me pulling out short and fast. This felt so damn good. All I could do was moan in response.

As he finger fucked me, he gently licked my clit with the tip of his tongue. With each slow lick, he applied more and more pressure. I crossed my legs around his head trying to use my legs as leverage so I wouldn't scream. As he applied the necessary pressure to compliment the necessary stroke, he involved his lips. He tongue kissed my pussy like he was actually giving me a passionate kiss on the lips of my face. He used all his assets, his tongue, lips, and fingers. I moaned, squirmed, and enjoyed.

Jaz couldn't compare to this at all. I was fucking a boy now I'm fucking a grown ass man. My body went bananas. The feeling was brand new, and my reaction was brand new. I screamed, moaned, and scratched. I was about to cum. I'm about to cum. He stopped.

He pulled my shirt and bra off to reveal my B cup sized breasts. He sucked my breasts like he was searching for milk to drink. He gently licked the dark ring around my nipple. He gently and perfectly bit my nipple. As he bit my nipple, he caressed my other breast at the same time. He took his tongue and flipped my nipple up and down with the tip of his tongue. I grabbed his back digging my nails in trying not to scream, though my moans were almost loud enough. He switched nipples repeating the process.

When he was done with that, he slid up sucking on my neck using his tongue and his lips together in one continuous motion. Then he proceeded up my chin to my lips. We kissed passionately as he rubs his manhood against me. He unbuttoned and unzipped his pants. He pulled a condom out of his pocket, magnum of course. He put it on then injected his dick in me. He thrust long and hard. "Aagh! Shit!" I screamed in pleasure. He then long-stroked fast; beating it up. "Fuck! Oh! Shit!" I screamed as I scratched the hell out of his back. He went back to thrusting long and slow. "Mmm...damn girl," he whispered. I couldn't say anything. The only thing I could do was breathe hard. He continued thrusting like this for ten more minutes then he stopped.

He pulled out and turned me over onto my stomach. He lifted my ass in the air and injected me again. I grabbed the bed sheets as money slid to the ground. He thrust long and fast, long and fast. "Ah! Fuck!" I screamed and continued, "Ah! Shit!...Shit!"

I tried to reach for something to grab onto but there wasn't anything to grab. My legs shook. *No! No! Not right now*, I said to myself. I didn't want to have an orgasm right now. I wanted this to last forever. I've never had sex like this before. *"Damn!"* I said to myself. I had a major orgasm, one that stopped my breathing temporarily.

I trembled; my entire body trembled. My entire body felt numb as sweat poured down my face and stripped my perm. Jasper would have been done a long time ago, but this man was still in me. Rome still thrusted me all the while I kept having orgasm after orgasm.

Finally, he came. To my surprise, his dick was still hard. Damn! I didn't know if I could take another round. However, Rome didn't hesitate to begin round 2. He buried his head in my pussy. He ate it from behind. He grabbed my thighs putting them over his shoulders. He stuck his tongue in and out of my pussy while rubbing my clitoris with his fingers. I couldn't do anything, except enjoy and moan loud enough to wake the dead.

He stopped then flipped me on over onto my back. He climbed off of the bed standing on the edge. He grabbed my legs pulling me to the edge of the bed. He rubbed his dick up and down my pussy gently while staring into my eyes. I stared at him with an expression of love because I loved every minute of this. Rome put the head of his dick in and thrust deep and slow. He grabbed my legs wrapping them around him. He put his entire nine inch dick inside of me. He held my ass in the air as he thrust fast, deep, and hard. "Ah! Shit! Ah! Shit! Aw!" I screamed in pleasure. "Rome! Rome!" I screamed. He kept beating and beating. The more he thrust the more I screamed. He kept hitting it while holding onto my thighs as my ass was slightly in the air. I tried to reach for him, so I could lock onto his back, but he was too far away. I couldn't reach him. My legs shook again. I had another orgasm. He was still beating hard, deep, and fast. I had a second orgasm then he pulled out. He lied on top of me. I wrapped my arms around him holding him tight. Sweat ran down his face and all over his back and chest. He lied on top of me for a few seconds then he slid the condom off.

"You alright?" He asked.

"Better than you know."

Rome put his finger inside of me slowly injecting it in and out, "I can do this all night."

"I…see."

"So what now?"

"What do you mean?" I questioned.

"I don't want to stop fucking you."

"Me either."

I gave Rome a very passionate kiss. He rolled over on his back. I kissed his chiseled chest. He continued to finger fuck me, and we continued to have a secret love affair.

Mahki

Introduction

The glow from the street light penetrated the opened window illuminating her golden complexion making it appear wet as she lied atop Mahki's wine-colored satin sheets stomach down. Her firm yet perfectly round behind reflected the light as Mahki gently ran her fingertips, fluttering, against the crest. The tickling sensation caused Jessica to giggle sexily as she pierced Mahki from the corner of her low upturned eyes. The dark-brown color of Jessica's eyes appeared light amber as the streetlight shone across them. Mahki licked her lips biting down on the bottom, her jet black eyes low speaking a language only Jessica could decipher.

Mahki climbed onto the bed as Jessica stared intently into her jet black eyes and rolled over onto her back. Mahki slowly licked Jessica from her inner ankle up to her vaginal lips as her hand gently slid up the inside of the other leg. Jessica slightly spread her legs in response. Mahki bypassed the vagina licking across the waistline and massaging it with her lips. She nibbled down Jessica's other leg with soft sensual bites stopping at the inside of her ankle.

She peered up at Jessica with her eyes low and her mid-back length jet black hair covering the side of her face. She slowly crawled on top of Jessica gently biting her chin then made her way to her lips. She kissed Jessica passionately as Jessica's hands gripped and caressed her back in circular motions. Mahki gently rubbed the up and down the back of Jessica's neck with cuffed hand; fingers on one side and the thumb on the other moving in slow circular motions as she applied more and more pressure with each movement. As they continued to kiss, Mahki grinded against Jessica as she wrapped her legs around her throwing it back. Makhi move her hands up the back of Jessica's shoulder length dark brown hair tugging on it. Jessica scratched across Mahki's shoulders as Mahki moaned in response.

They continued grinding against one another as Mahki massaged Jessica's neck with her lips; going up and down then across and up and down the other side. As she kissed Jessica's neck, she slid her hands up both of Jessica's arms locking fingers with hers pinning her to the bed and she grinded more forcefully.

Mahki released Jessica's hands moving down to her 'c' cup size breasts. Mahki licked the nipple in a circular motion with the tip of her tongue then closed her lips around the erect nipple gently grazing it with her teeth. Jessica whispered, "Shit," as she gripped Mahki's hair squirming a bit. Mahki massaged the other breast with her hand as she sucked on Jessica's nipple like she was nursing. Jessica squirmed pulling

Mahki's hair in response to the electrifying sensation. She said, "Mmmm," as her body tensed.

Mahki kissed across Jessica's chest and repeated on the other nipple. As she sucked her Jessica's nipple, she slid her fingers in between her vaginal lips rubbing up and down. Jessica pulled her hair again and said, "Daaammmn…shit." Mahki injected two fingers into her with her fingers curled upwards sliding them in and out slowly as she forcefully tapped the g-spot. Jessica pulled her hair yet again and said, "Got damn…shiiiiittttt."

The alarm on Mahki's cell phone sounded. With her arms folded across her head as a pillow, she popped her head up momentarily forgetting she was in the break room at work. Her cheeks and tips of her ears were red as she inhaled and exhaled slowly trying to come down from her dream. Her notebook rested in front of her as she still held the pen in her right hand. She rubbed her eye with her left hand then stared down at the notebook re-reading what she had written before she dosed off. It read:

Every thought is like a whisper; imagining the warmth of your breath massaging my ear
Remembering the soft touch of your skin as my fingers slipped between yours; an electrifying sensation that provoked a little fear
An intense stare that has me envisioning our souls intertwined as one in a forbidden dance
Floating on the same vibration; a frequency of intensive passion unto the spiritual as our bodies are in a sacred trance

*To give and receive, to give and receive; building the foundation for a
lifetime of prosperity as we engage in a love unlike another
Wanting to explore your mind, caress your heart, and whisper a language
to your soul like a melody specifically played for one another
The sound of your voice echoes, it echoes, it echoes, vibrating my rhyme and
rhythm like a blues in your thighs
Wanting to make your body explode like contorted schisms; breathlessness
as satisfaction is reflected in your eyes
To kiss, to bite, to scratch, to embrace, to love every inch of your physical
being
Your mind is more addictive than crack; tunnel vision — no one but you is
what I'm seeing
Like a CD that skips saying the same thing thrice
You tore down my walls the moment you entered my life
Every thought is like a whisper; imagining the warmth of your breath
massaging my ear
Remembering the soft touch of your skin as my fingers slipped between
yours; an electrifying sensation that made everything clear…
…It's you and only you I want to behold…
…I want you; mind, body, heart, and soul…*

Roger peeked his head in the break room and said, "Dr. Ng (pronounced 'ing'). The board is waiting."

While closing her notebook, she said, "Coming."

Same Sex

Mahki peered through her high power electron microscope in the lab she worked in studying the response of a new medication she created for harmful bacteria. She glanced up at the clock and sighed. Dr. Smith said, "You look flustered."

"Can't hide anything, hun?" She shook her head in disapproval then continued, "I thought I had it."

Dr. Smith walked towards her and said, "Let me take a look," he peeked into the microscope, "It's eating them up. I say good job."

"That's the problem. It's eating up *all* of the cells…even healthy tissue. This shit is toxic."

Dr. Smith giggled, "Shit? Yeah, you're stressed. Don't worry. This is a great start. We'll get the grant."

Mahki didn't say anything in response. She stared at Jessica through the window in the laboratory talking to another employee. Jessica worked in another area because she was not a Doctor or Laboratory Technician she was a grant writer, so she worked in the business office on the other side of the Lab. She wore a light gray business suit with some black heels and a black satin button down shirt underneath. Dr.

Smith glanced at Mahki then peered out of the window at Jessica. He said, "I don't know why you two are still playing these games."

Mahki turned to him, "What?"

"It's obvious to me that the two of you are crazy about each other."

Mahki squinted her eyes, "You think she's crazy about me? How?"

"Everything, the way she breaks her neck to come over here when she works on the other side of the building, the way she looks at you when you're not looking. You need to make that happen."

Mahki removed the side from the microscope and placed it into a box that contained other slides. She turned the power off on the microscope, "Nah, that's my best friend. Besides, that doesn't mean she likes me…and she has a girlfriend."

"Does she love her?"

"I suppose so. I don't know. I've never asked her. I just know they've been together for close to six months now."

Dr. Smith smirked, "My wife had a boyfriend when I met her. Guess who won." He giggled.

"I'm not a home wrecker. Besides, crossing that line could mess things up. Just think, if it doesn't work out, I could lose my best friend of ten years. Not worth it. I'd rather have my friend."

"So you're telling me you haven't thought about it?"

"I've had a lot of thoughts but none of them pertained to being in a relationship with my best friend. I don't want a relationship with anyone. You know I'm as free as a bird. Relationships feel like I'm in chains and shackles. Ugh. Y'all can have that."

Dr. Smith smirked and he shook his head in disapproval as he moved closer to the window peering out at Jessica. He admired her physique: five feet eight, 160 lbs tones, perfect hourglass figure, dimples so deep they could be seen when she talked, medium brown complexion, and a perfect behind. He said, "Look at that…Mmm…Mmm…Mmm. You haven't at least thought about having sex with her?"

"Of course I have…I'm a woman who likes women. Almost every good-looking woman I come across I think about sexually…Look Mike…just let it go. I'm not sleeping with or being in a relationship with my best friend. It's simply not going to happen."

"All right…but sometimes the best relationships occur between friends and sometimes the other person feels the same way. You should at least ask her. Best friends make the best lovers. My wife is my best friend."

"Bye Mike."

"See you Monday you mule," he walked out of the lab.

Mahki peered out of the window again. Jessica glanced over, smiled, and waved. Mahki waved in response.

Jessica came into the lab as Mahki was cleaning everything up preparing to leave. Jessica said in her smooth smoky tone, "Did you forget about tonight?"

Mahki's eyebrows frowned, "I guess I did. What's tonight?"

"It's the thirteenth. You were supposed to join me for dinner, remember?" Jessica slowly approached Mahki as her heels clucked with each slow step.

"I had no idea it was the thirteenth. I just know it's Friday. You know I have issues remembering dates. I just know what day it is."

"Well, the reservation was for an hour ago."

Mahki glanced at the clock. It read 8:45 p.m. Her shift ended at 5 o'clock yet she was still working. "I'm sorry."

"I was *really* looking forward to this."

Mahki paused. *Did she say 'really'?* She thought. "Why is that? It's just dinner."

"Because we haven't spent much time together. You're always working. I just wanted to have you all to myself."

Mahki's hands trembled a bit and her heartbeat hastened. She was nervous, "Well…I can cook you dinner if you'd like. How's Carlita these days?"

Jessica smirked, "Who?"

"What do you mean? That is your girlfriend, correct?"

Jessica walked towards Mahki as the smell of her perfume made Mahki's pussy throb. She stood in front of her and said, "Notice anything missing?"

Mahki glanced around the laboratory. She was baffled, "No…not that I can see."

Jessica unzipped her purse pulling out Mahki's 8" x 5" notebook. She opened it and read, "The sound of your voice echoes, it echoes, it echoes, vibrating my rhyme and rhythm like a blues in your thighs. Wanting to make your body explode like contorted schisms; breathlessness as satisfaction is reflected in your eyes."

Mahki appeared a little embarrassed, "Wow…"

"You left this in the conference room. Who were you speaking of?"

Mahki didn't look at her, "It doesn't matter."

Jessica smirked, "You once told me that the sound of my voice is so soothing it echoes, it echoes like a rhyme and rhythm of a lullaby."

Mahki sat on top of the desk in the lab in silence with her head tiled down, "I did?"

"Yes, you did. It was four years ago when we were in Hawaii. I sang a song for the Captain."

"Oh…I can't believe you remember that," she mumbled, "'Cause I sure and the hell didn't."

As she approached Mahki, "So is this poem about me?"

"Do you want it to be about you?"

"You didn't answer my question," she smiled, "Why are you doing this Mahki? You know good and well you want me just as bad as I want you. Why do you deny it?"

"We're friends. You're my best friend; like sisters. I think we should leave things as they are," Mahki slid down from the desk then closed the blinds to the window in the lab that showed the hallway. Jessica followed her.

"That's your problem. You think too damn much. You're too fucking smart for your own good."

Mahki giggled, "Too smart for my own good?" She laughed then continued, "That doesn't make sense. How can anyone be too smart?"

"Why don't you stop thinking for just a moment…and feel something? It's like you're two people in one. The Mahki on paper says, 'Make love to me', whereas the Mahki in person says, 'Fuck love.'"

Mahki walked towards the set of windows on the wall that showed the outside of the building; a wonderful view of the parking lot; only two cars remained – she began closing the blinds, "Jessica, please. You know me better than anyone else. You know good and well that I don't do relationships."

"Did I say anything about a relationship?...Just be honest. If you're not attracted to me, then tell me that."

Mahki cut her eyes towards Jessica as she closed the last blind, "Did I say I wasn't attracted to you? Don't put words in my mouth. You know I don't like that."

"Then what is it? You've fucked all of your friends…except for me."

Mahki walked towards Jessica staring into her eyes standing three inches shorter than her. Jessica crossed her arms across her chest with her nose a little flared. Mahki said, "Because I respect you. Since I have a high degree of respect for you, I'm not going to treat you like I treat those bitches. What the hell do I look like speaking to you, groping you, and lying to you like I do them? I don't want a relationship, and the last thing I'd ever want to do is hurt you. I like to fuck whomever I want whenever I want, and the idea of settling down doesn't appeal to me right now."

Jessica snickered, "You think I want to settle down with you?"

Mahki appeared puzzled, "Well, isn't that where you are going with this?"

"No," she walked close into Mahki's face, "I want you to fuck me."

Mahki licked both of her lips then said, "If I fuck you, when you have those multiple full body orgasms rippling through you, and your back is arched, when you peer at the wall, you'll swear you see God."

Jessica placed her hands on Mahki's shoulders, "I want to see if you can back that up."

Mahki smirked, "This is cute...but..."

Jessica grabbed Mahki's face kissing her passionately. Mahki stepped backwards as Jessica walked with her still kissing her. Before she knew it, Mahki had her back to the wall as Jessica pressed her pelvis against hers still kissing her. Mahki rubbed her hands up and down the sides of Jessica's waistline and hips. She pulled away from the kiss and bit down on Jessica's shoulder. Jessica mumbled, "Shit." Mahki gently pushed Jessica away from her as the tips of her ears and her cheeks were red. She said, "You started it. Don't fall in love."

Jessica smirked as she licked her lips and slid her suit jacket off while kicking her heels off. She unbuttoned her shirt revealing a black lace bra. Mahki sucked on her bottom lip as she slowly approached Jessica. She rubbed her hand from the side of her neck down the middle of her chest to her pants line. She unbuttoned Jessica's pants and put her hand in her panties. She rubbed the knuckle of her index finger up and down the vaginal split. She mumbled, "You're so wet…Mmmm." Jessica stared down at Mahki and kissed her. They kissed passionately as Jessica slid her shirt off. Mahki kept rubbing Jessica's clit with her two fingers in circular motions applying more and more pressure. Jessica said, "Ooooh…Oooooh…Shiiiiitttt."

Mahki removed her hand from Jessica's pants licking her two fingers. She picked Jessica up and carried her towards the desk laying her on top of it. She licked across her pants line moving her tongue in quick circular motions as she massaged her breasts with her hands. Mahki bit down on the side of Jessica's waistline and nibbled up to her lower bra line then licked across the bra line and nibbled down the other side biting down on her waistline. Jessica squirmed as she tried not to make a sound. Mahki climbed onto the desk with one knee in between Jessica's legs and the other to her left side kissing and licking up the middle of her abdomen towards her bra line. As she approached the bra line, she gently slid her hands to the side of Jessica's torso wrapping them around her back unhooking her bra. She slowly slid the bra off tossing it to the crème tiled floor.

Mahki wrapped her mouth around Jessica's nipple and breathed on it while she flicked the other erect nipple with the tip of her fingernail in a quick up and down motion; fluttering. Jessica squirmed pulling her hair, "Shhhhhiiiiiitttt," she said with her teeth clenched. Mahki gently bit Jessica's nipple scraping it with her teeth as her lips enclosed and sucked, then with her tongue, she moved it around in slow circular motions as she continued to stroke the other nipple with her fingernails. Jessica gripped her hair tightly, "Oooooh!" Mahki licked across to the other nipple and repeated the same process.

Mahki opened her mouth and breathed down the middle of Jessica's abdomen towards her pants line. She licked swiftly back and forth across the panty line. She unzipped Jessica's slacks, removing her pants and underwear, carefully tossing them onto the floor. She placed each hand onto Jessica's knees and rubbed up as she licked the inside of her left thigh in small circular motions. When she got to the pussy, she stuck her tongue in the vagina flipping it up and down then licked up the middle of her hairless lips.

Mahki moved her tongue around the clit in circular motions applying more and more pressure. Jessica tensed up as her legs wrapped around Mahki. Mahki opened her mouth and took a sip of her juices as she motioned her tongue up and down. "Ooooooh…Mmmm," Jessica moaned. Mahki flicked her tongue up and down quickly on the clit. Jessica pulled her hair and shouted, "Oh Shit!" Mahki tongue kissed the clit, sucking, blowing, licking, kissing, as she bobbed her head up and down. Jessica's legs locked on her and her back arced as she pulled her hair with every sensation while moaning.

As Mahki continued to eat the pussy, she rubbed her finger around the inside of Jessica's vagina trying to stretch it out a little. She injected two fingers going in and out slowly making sure she forcefully tapped the g-spot every time she entered. Jessica went from moaning to shouting, "Uh…Uh…Ooooooh…Shit…Got damn." Mahki injected her faster and faster with each stroke as she tongue kissed the clit. She continued this as Jessica screamed and shouted until her back arced and legs locked tightly around Mahki's head. Mahki kept sucking on her clit like a baby sucks on a bottle. Jessica's waste jerked uncontrollably as her entire body trembled. Mahki kept sucking on her clit. Jessica's waist and shoulders jerked as Jessica screamed. Mahki released her as Jessica kept jerking and was almost completely out of breath. Jessica whispered, "I can't take anymore." Jessica kept cumming as Mahki stood watching. Mahki sat on the desk and ran her fingers through Jessica's hair. She gave her a gentle peck then said, "Are you all right?" Jessica was speechless. She hugged Mahki and giggled, "Let's…do this again…at your place."

One Month Prior...

Tyvid, Geena, and Justice sat in the lobby at the Gynecologist's office. They waited to be seen for their yearly Pap test. Tyvid sat with her legs crossed reading a magazine dressed like she's on her way to a club. She had on a pair of skin-tight hip-hugger jeans, a pair of open toe high heels, and a tight fitting shirt showing her cleavage. Geena stared out of the window appearing bored. Her attire screamed, "I'm a mother." She had a plain Jane appearance. Justice was dressed for a business meeting while ignoring the free world and organizing her PDA.

The receptionist yelled, "Justice Moorse." Justice was so into what she was doing she didn't hear her. The receptionist browsed the room with her eyes then called out, "Is there a Justice Moorse in here?"

Tyvid pulled the magazine down from in front of her face peering at the other women, "Which one of y'all is Justice Moorse?"

"Not me!" Geena stated.

Justice sat silently in her own world. Tyvid walked to Justice tapping her leg, "Excuse me, Justice? The front desk wants you."

"Oh! Thank you," Justice said while standing then walking towards the reception desk.

As Justice walked to the reception desk, Tangeray walked in. She had on a bright pink and white Capri outfit with white and bright pink gym shoes. Her nails were long and colorful. Her hair was peppered with bright red weaved streaks beyond the shoulders. She stood behind Justice waiting her turn.

"There is a $50 co-pay for this visit," The receptionist mentioned.

"$50! Damn! What insurance you got? You need to turn that in and get you some Medicaid girl," Tangeray blurts.

While pulling a $50 bill out of her wallet and handing it to the receptionist, "I make too much money for Medicaid."

"Well, excuse me miss high and mighty," Tangeray responded.

"I'll get you a receipt," The receptionist stated as she stepped away from the desk.

"Okay!" Justice said then continued typing on her PDA.

"What you do for a living?" Tangeray asked.

"I own my own public relations firm," Justice explained.

"Oh! Must be nice," Tangeray said.

Justice continued typing on her PDA. Tangeray stood behind her feeling very impatient.

"Damn! Can this bitch be any slower?" Tangeray said.

Justice smirked, "Tell me about it. I've been coming here since I was 15 and each visit they get slower."

They both stood there another five minutes. Tangeray motioned Justice to move out of her way and said, "Excuse me."

Justice stepped away from the window. Tangeray stepped up banging on the window, "Hey! Hey!"

Geena stared at Tangeray shaking her head in disapproval and said, "Ahh! Another one of these. I really need to switch doctors."

Tyvid giggled in agreement.

The receptionist returned to the window, "Don't bang on the glass," she asserted.

Tangeray placed her hand on her hip and responded, "Well, can you hurry up? How long does it take to print out a damn receipt? I've been standing here for 15 minutes."

"I apologize for the inconvenience, but we are running a little behind. There is only one doctor here and all of the rooms are full. Just hand me your medical card and sign in. I'll call you," the receptionist explained.

"Nah! I'll sign in right here and you bring my card right back. I don't get another one until next month. I can't afford to lose that one," Tangeray demanded.

Tangeray gave the receptionist the information. The receptionist walked away from the window. Tangeray reached in the window grabbing the clipboard. She signed in on the sign-in sheet and began filling out the intake form on the clipboard. The receptionist returned handing Justice her receipt and medical card. Justice walked away from the window sitting five seats away from Geena. The receptionist made a copy of Tangeray's medical card. She immediately returned Tangeray her medical card in fear that she might become irate. Tangeray completed the intake form and took a seat in the row behind Tyvid.

Tyvid burst out laughing. All of the women glanced over at her. She got silent then she burst out laughing again. Mahki walked into the doctor's office. She wore her lab coat because she was coming from work.

Tangeray stared at Tyvid then said, "What are you laughing at?"

Tyvid pulled the magazine down from in front of her face, "This article. Oh! My God! This is some funny shit. I feel for these women. I really do."

"You really read those? What does it say?" Tangeray said while getting up and sitting three seats away from Tyvid in the same row.

"It's talking about women who are not sexually satisfied. This one girl is comedy."

Geena joined the conversation, "There's nothing funny about that at all."

Tangeray laughed, "You must be one of the one's who ain't satisfied."

Mahki sat down across from Justice.

"I'm not saying that. I'm just saying you gotta feel for a woman who never gets her rocks off," Geena stated.

Justice joined in, "Damn right! What's the point of making love if you don't get anything out of it?"

Tyvid said, "That's why you shouldn't make love. Love is completely overrated. That's most women's problems. You want to be loved too much. Hold me, touch me, love me. I'll tell any woman, if you want to get off, stop making love and start fucking."

"That's the dumbest thing I ever heard", Mahki said then continued, "It doesn't matter if you're making love or just fucking. Sex is more mental than physical. The attraction factor is a major key in good sex. The more turned on you are the better the sex will be."

"Nah! That's not it. My husband is fine as he wants to be, and I'm still not satisfied. In the beginning it was great, now I'm bored," Geena added.

"That's what I'm talking about here ladies," while pointing at Geena and continuing, "She is in love and is still not satisfied. You know why because there's no thrill. There's no element of surprise. Your husband is predictable now," Tyvid explained.

"So what you're an expert on sex? Please! You cannot believe everything you read in those magazines. Whether in love or not, if someone can put it down he or she can put it down. Lovemaking is an art. Sorry, but everybody isn't an artist. That's as simple as it gets," Makhi stated.

"What is your name?" Tangeray asked.

"Mahki."

"Well, Mahki please shut the hell up. We want to hear what she has to say," Tangeray blurted.

"What?" Makhi said in offense to Tangeray's statement.

"No disrespect, but this isn't a debate. This subject interests me. I work 60 hours a week, give or take a few. It takes time to fall in love, and I don't have that much free time.

My biological clock is ticking. I want to hear this without any objections…Please," Justice confessed.

"So do I. 'Cause my man got a big dick and still can't fuck. I need to get mine off. So explain girl explain", Tangeray blurted.

"Suit yourself. I'm not partaking in this conversation," Mahki replied.

"Well, don't! Go ahead girl. What was you saying?" Tangeray said.

"How is fucking better than making love?" Geena inquired.

"It's not better. It's freakier. You don't have any attachment to that person. You don't love him, and he's not your man. Since you never fucked him before, you have the element of surprise. On top of that, the naughtiness of it heightens your arousal," Tyvid enlightened.

"How?" Geena asked.

"Why do you think men cheat? It's not because they are not in love with their woman. Cheating is freakier because it's something they know they're not supposed to do. It's naughty. On top of that, the sex is unpredictable leaving an element of surprise. Getting away with it gives him a rush or a thrill. When it comes to sex, if you put naughtiness, unpredictability, and thrill together, it equals good sex. You get off simply because you know it's wrong," Tyvid explicated.

"I'm impressed. That actually makes a little sense," Mahki complimented.

"I thought you weren't in this convo anymore," Tangeray stated.

"I'm not. I'm just agreeing with her point," Mahki said.

"Then stay out of it!" Tangeray demanded.

Mahki leaned up in her seat and said, "Where do you get off..."

Geena cut her off, "Ladies enough! Control yourselves. We are all adults here. No more insults! Damn!"

Mahki stood from her seat with an angry expression upon her face. She sat away from the group. Tangeray rolled her eyes at Mahki but sat quietly.

"So you saying if I do something I know I shouldn't do, I'll get off sexually?" Justice asked.

"Yes! That's like a man getting turned on by sleeping with two women at the same time. Them touching one another turns him on because it's wrong. Just like a good girl being with a bad boy. He's unpredictable, he's naughty, and he's a thrill. In the eyes of society, he's wrong for her," Tyvid added.

The receptionist called out, "Geena Perado. Room 3."

While getting up, "Damn! I have to go. Nice talking with you ladies."

They all said, "Nice talking to you too."

"Girl, remember to fuck. Don't make love anymore. I am writing an article about the advice I'm giving y'all. Trust me. I know what I'm talking about," Tyvid offered.

"I'll give it some thought," Geena said then walked to her examining room.

The ladies continued their conversation.

"I'm not saying become a whore, but stop making love. Fuck somebody at least once in your life. Honestly speaking ladies, which turns you on more? When a man says baby tonight I'm going to make the sweetest love to you? Or when a man says baby I'm 'bout to fuck the shit out of you?" Tyvid asked.

Tangeray added, "The second one."

"I heard that!" Justice screamed.

Mahki smirked in agreement.

"Now ladies stop fantasizing and do what you really want to do. Make one of your fantasies become reality, at least once in your life. I bet money that your satisfaction is guaranteed," Tyvid advised then continued, "If not, I'll be reading an article about you next."

"You won't be reading about me. I'm not dumb enough to put my business on national display," Mahki enlightened from across the room.

"Me either," Tangeray agreed.

Justice stared at Tyvid and said, "Have you ever made any of your fantasies a reality?"

"All the time," Tyvid admitted.

"So you telling me that your man satisfies you every single time?" Tangeray asked.

"I don't have a man anymore. I've been happily divorced for three years now, and I've had the best sex of my life within these three years. Hello!" Tyvid replied.

"What about you Mahki? Does your man please you every single time without disappointment?" Tangeray inquired.

"I don't have a man," Mahki confessed.

"A girlfriend?" Tangeray blurted.

Mahki said, "That's none of your business."

"Well, it is that day and age. Enquiring minds wanted to know," Tangeray said.

"I don't have a girlfriend," Mahki assured.

"Any man friends?" Tangeray questioned.

"No!" Mahki stated.

"Well, how do you get off?" Justice asked.

"Use your imagination," Mahki mumbled in a 'duh' manner.

"You nasty bitch! See I knew it. Smart bitches are the biggest freaks," Tangeray assaulted.

Mahki laughed, "You have no idea."

The receptionist returned to the window and yelled, "Tyvid Cane, Room 10."

"I'm coming," Tyvid said as she stood from her seat. Tyvid laid the magazine down on the chair next to her.

Tangeray grabbed it and said, "Oh! I'm taking this with me."

Tyvid smiled grabbing her purse, "Give fucking a try. If you are afraid to do it physically, you can always pretend. Read my article in next months's edition of *Lustful Minds*. I'm going to leave the magazine wide open so you can go directly to my article. Follow the directions thoroughly. I promise it will open your eyes and motivate you to stop making love and start fucking."

Mahki replied, "I'll be sure to look for that article this time next month."

Justice stated, "Me too."

Tyvid said, "I hope so." She walked to the examination room.

The Article

Lustful Minds
Page 54
Reasons to Have More Sex and More Orgasms
Tyvid Cane
November 21, 2014

The thought or idea of having a lot of sex outside of the union of marriage has been looked down upon for many centuries. To have multiple partners, to have sex without being married, to have sex without being in a relationship, remains a forbidden and detestable act; a sort of taboo in western society. Most people are told to wait to have sex until they are in a committed, loving relationship while others are taught to hold out until marriage. Morally, these teachings are correct. However, the people that preached this type of abstinence or celibacy are clearly unaware of the health benefits of having sex, especially the benefits of having orgasms.

Unfortunately, only 25% of women actually reach orgasms each time they have sex from penetration. The clitoris is the part of the female reproductive system responsible for orgasms not the g-spot as often speculated which is why good oral sex is imperative for the stimulation of mind-blowing orgasms in women. Some women report having female ejaculations (squirting) and believe that is an orgasm. However, they have sadly mistaken. An ejaculation is not an orgasm. With an orgasm, the clitoris, vagina, and sometimes the anus, contract and pulsates intensely multiple times as the brain releases a chemical called oxytocin which induces feelings of relaxation – hence why people feel sleepy after a good orgasm.

There are many health benefits for having orgasm. They include: 1) orgasms help insomniacs sleep better by relaxing the body and mind, 2) orgasm increases people's tolerance to pain due to the brain releasing oxytocins and endorphins which are the body's natural pain relievers, 3) orgasms help stimulate the brain due to an increase in blood flow, 4) orgasms are a great way to relieve stress due to oxytocin inducing feelings of relaxation, 5) orgasms boost the immune system, 6) orgasms boost estrogen levels helping to prevent heart disease and osteoporosis, 7) orgasms improve digestion and helps prevent cancer, 8) orgasm improves confidence and mood, 9) orgasms increases the hormone DHEA in the brain which improves brain function and promotes healthy skin, 10) orgasms cures migraines, and 11) helps prevent people from cheating, etc. It's also been speculated that orgasms increases people's life spans and get better as you age.

Sex is a beautiful thing especially when shared with two people that love each other. However, if you're having sex or making love and you are not having orgasms, there is no health benefit for the act and really…what's the point?…Single women, stop trying to be the "good girl" or the "virtuous woman" waiting for her husband or wife. By doing so, you are missing out on the health benefits and the pleasure of the female orgasm. Stop living a fantasy inside of your head and start fucking…but above all be safe and protect yourself. Married women and committed relationship women…it's time to have more sex and time to have more orgasms.

My name is Tyvid Cane and I approve this advice.

Chosen – Chapter One

Glossy, tired eyes reflected the large curtain-less window like a mirror. Rays of light, bright yet concentrated dimmed in response to the setting sun. The colorful foot-prints across the sky left thin trails of clouds soon to disappear within the darkness of the night. Jordin, a second year senior, and victim of the surrealism of her own mind, crept toward the window. Her black high heel biker boots clucked and echoed with every slow step.

Her breath continuously fogged the window then dissipated a few seconds later. Her long dark brown hair eclipsed her line of sight as she tucked it behind her ear to no avail. Her hair slipped from the comfort of the crease where the ear attached to her head eclipsing her line of sight yet again. Blowing her hair out of her face she held her hair up as a temporary ponytail holder. She turned and quickly looked behind her. The cold silence in the hallway raised the hairs on the back of her neck.

Jordin turned to the window and peered out, as she always did, removing her hair from blocking her line of sight yet again. Michael stood outside of the residence hall speaking with some students. His hair cut short and his face had no facial hair with droopy yet bright eyes. Jordin's eyes protruded and her heart rate hastened. She held her breath as she stepped out of sight pinning herself against the wall the window posted. Her hands trembled as she gripped her purse tightly. She peered out of the window. Michael had vanished.

The elevator dinged loudly echoing in the silence of the hallway starling Jordin. The elevator doors opened as Mira stepped out. Jordin remained pinned against the wall as her breathing was shallow and rapid. The elevator doors closed.

Mira asked, "Jordin are you okay? You look terrified."

Jordin giggled, "Nah girl, I'm fine. I'm just tripping, you know?" She peaked out of the window again.

Mira temporarily rested her hand on her hip, "You went to that sorority party didn't you?"

Jordin stared into her pale blue eyes, "Yeah, why?"

Mira caught her purse from slipping from the crest of her shoulder trying not to drop the two textbooks she held firmly within her grasp, "Rumor is someone laced the drinks with PCP. A girl at the party was rushed to emergency. You might wanna get checked out. PCP causes hallucinations."

Jordin smacked her lips as her sharply arched eye brows grimaced, "For real? I didn't hear about that," her smoky voice dryly muttered.

Mira rescued her long frizzy sandy brown hair from underneath the strap of her pink purse then flung it across the back of her shoulders, "It's true. Been buzzing around campus all morning. There's gonna to be an investigation."

Jordin glanced away from Mira, "Thanks for lettin' me know."

"You missed the elevator. Are you going down?"

Jordin glanced out of the window, "Eventually. Trying to make sure I have everything."

Mira raised her eyebrow and nodded her head, "Guess I'll see you later."

Jordin nodded her head in agreement. Mira walked down the short stretch of the hallway before turning the corner on her way to her dorm room. Her two inch high heels hollowed as they clucked the floor with each shallow step.

Jordin peered out of the window again catching her hair from blinding her in search of Michael. Where did he go? How did he know? She didn't see him anywhere as her heart rate slowed and her muscles relaxed. She gave a sigh of relief as she rubbed the back of her neck smirking. She combed her hair with her fingers then gently rubbed her eyes without smearing her bronze eye shadow as she collected herself, *I'm scaring myself. I need to calm the fuck down.* She popped her neck then her knuckles then pressed the down button on the elevator.

An unfamiliar girl stood next to her. Her clothes dirty, ragged, and smelled exceedingly bad; a mixture of underarm funk and trash. Her hair was ear length, slicked back, and dirty. The girl's non-arched eye brows, droopy eyes, and sharp features gave her a masculine appeal. Jordin knew the girl was not a student but felt pity for her although she secretly wondered where she came from. She cleared her throat, "I have some long johns, some sweat clothes, and a quilt if you need to stay warm out there."

The girl stood without saying one word; her body rigid and cold; her attention towards the floor. Jordin slyly scratched her nose with her hand covering her entire nose, "Well unh…I have a couple dollars if you hungry."

The girl didn't say anything, an awkward silence. The only sounds in the hall were the girl's heavy breathing and muffled voices from people talking loudly in the dorms down the hall. Jordin cleared her throat, "Going down?"

Dorm room doors slammed shut as Jordin's muscles tensed. The girl stared blankly at the elevator in an inexpressive tone, "Cheaters always win but whores pay the price."

Jordin grimaced stepping away from the girl towards the window, "Excuse me?"

The girl grabbed Jordin's arm and yanked her towards her; nose to nose. She mumbled in a deep, masculine voice, "You." She snarled.

Jordin screamed, snatched her arm from the girl, pushed her down then ran down the end of the hall opposite the dead end of the window she stood next to. The girl chased her as the elevator dinged and the doors opened.

Jordin ran down the hall continuously looking behind. The girl bent down on all fours, hands and feet, behind her as her green eyes turned black. The lights in the hall flickered then dimmed. Jordin ran hastily as her clacking footsteps clacked three times every second filling the silence of the hall. As she looked behind, the girl climbed on the wall and ran behind her quickly moving like a cheetah. She opened her mouth revealing sharp teeth like that of a shark as saliva dribbled from her mouth while she roared like a male lion.

Jordin turned the corner of the "L" shaped hallway coasting down the longest hall towards the stairway clenching her purse. The girl turned the corner behind her on the wall. She ran down the wall onto the floor leveled with Jordin.

Jordin burst through the exit door passed the other set of elevators. The door smacked the wall as she missed the first step tumbling down the first level of stairs bumbling and fumbling landing on her side. She slid against the wall of the landing opposite the doorway. She dropped her purse and cell phone. Stiff, bruised, and achy, she got up and ran, limping, down the second level of stairs skipping steps - cluck, cluck, cluck, every second. The girl leaped down the entire first level of the asymmetrical "u" shaped staircase onto the landing like a flying squirrel; thudding as she kept her balance. Jordin sighed as her eyes moved frantically.

Jordin hopped down the stairs onto the landing with the girl only a half of flight behind her. The girl's footsteps sounded sticky and wet. Jordin soared down all of the stairs from the landing onto the next floor, stumbling as she landed. The girl ascended down behind her onto the landing on all fours. Jordin erupted out of the exit doors onto the second floor. The girl flew down the second level of stairs from the landing as the exit door swung closed and smacked her. She fluttered backwards as she flipped onto the steps on her side. She quickly sprung onto all fours, growled loudly in irritation, stood on her two feet, and ripped out of the door.

Jordin ran through the second floor banging on doors, "Help…Please help me! Someone help me please!" She heard a few doors slam shut ahead of her. Several people beat on their dorm room doors shouting because they could not open the doors. The girl continued in pursuit of Jordin. Jordin continuously glanced back as the girl gained on her. As fast as she was capable of making her legs move with her injury, she galloped down the long stretch of the "L" shaped hallway towards the elevator.

Jordin breathed heavy and fast temporarily forgetting her training. Her heart seemed to flutter as sweat dripped from the tip of her nose and brow. The lights flickered continuously and sounds like animal growls were all that held her attention, the sounds got closer and closer, more and more audible. Hairs all over her body stood erect. Tears swelled as Jordin's hazel eyes moved frantically. *I'm stuck.* She realized she had no way out; no escape from this insane, inhumane woman. She couldn't make it down another flight of stairs.

Jordin turned the corner of the "L" shaped hallway onto the shorter hallway so quickly she broke her heel, twisted her ankle, fell, and slid against the wall. The pain rippled through her body like a shockwave. "Aaaaagh!" She wailed. The adrenaline dump caused her to ignore the pain and immediately stand. She ran with a serious limp towards the elevator. The girl turned the corner behind her gaining on her quickly; eight feet…, seven feet…, six feet…, and closing. The elevator dinged. Jordin made it her business to catch it at all costs.

Michael stepped out of the elevator as she approached. She gasped. She attempted to stop so she could turn and run the other way. Panicking, and not being rational, her first thought was to run away from Michael without considering she was running towards the inhumane girl, but placed too much weight on her twisted ankle, stumbled to the floor on her side, and slid into the wall. Michael stepped around Jordin as she slid into the wall. The girl continued to run after Jordin despite Michael's presence. After smacking the wall, Jordin crawled to the elevator. She reached her arm out sticking her hand in between the doors before they completely closed. The doors opened. She crawled into the elevator. The doors closed then took her down.

Fluid Veracity - Prologue

Loud sirens faded in and out as I faded in and out of consciousness. The voices sounded muffled, and I couldn't quite make out what was being said. My eyes opened wide as I stared into the Paramedic's face. His tanned complexion, steel gray eyes, and good looks should have had a calming effect on me as he revealed a false smirk; I noticed the nervousness in his eyes. My mother frantically yelled words I could not hear. Her normally mocha complexion appeared light caramel as her eyes moved here and there almost uncontrollably. The Paramedic placed an oxygen mask over my nose and mouth, and I could feel my heart struggling to beat in my chest; slow and weak. Tears drizzled from my eyes as I spoke silently to God. *Please don't let me die. Lord, I am begging you to please show mercy on me.*

I cried tears of blood as the doors of the ambulance opened. The gurney I was strapped dropped out of the ambulance and rolled away as another set of doors miraculously opened. I was blinded by the abundance of hazy lights that gleamed from the ceiling of the emergency room. The Paramedics surrounded me, running me towards the nearest triage as I attempted to remain calm during this bumpy ride. Every sound was hollow and echoed as my gurney was wheeled into Triage number two. I was alarmed at the amount of people that ran to my aid; doctors, nurses, and others. I couldn't count them if I tried; they kept moving about. My mother held my hand assuring me that I would make it through. She continuously told me to fight. She said, "Fight baby. No matter what, fight."

The doctors switched me from the gurney to the bed as my mother's hand slowly broke away. I turned my head towards my mother, confused because I had no idea what was going on and how I wound up here. I searched silently for answers as I took a glimpse of the gurney. It was full of blood like something off of a gory horror film, only it was real life and not a movie. Panicking, I quickly examined myself; I was covered in blood. The blood was so dark it almost appeared black. With a pair of shears, the doctor cut the clothes from my body. He walked passed my mother as though she was invisible; she was a ghost to him. My eyes locked with my mother's eyes as I noticed, for the first time, how worried she really was. I could see my reflection in my mother's dark brown eyes and the tears she desperately tried to prevent from escaping.

One of the doctor's, a medical intern I supposed, asked me for my name. The sound of his voice echoed like it continuously bounced off of a concave wall. I attempted to state my name but was unsure of what name I gave him because I could not hear myself speak. It was like someone tossed me into a black and white closed caption movie without caption. Everything and everybody were moving in slow motion as I felt a painful pinch in the fold of my right arm. I blanked out then back in.

When I blanked out, I had a flash of a dark-skinned woman but couldn't make out her facial features. She seemed possessed by the way her eyebrows grumbled and her nose flared. The white conjunctivas of her eyes were pink as she had the most hateful expression on her face like a devil. She was six inches away from my face violently yelling and screaming at me. I paused trying so hard to remember, "Pow!" The sound of a gunshot rang in my ears as it echoed. I remembered. I finally remembered. At this point, I remembered. I leaned up and screamed, "Save my baby. Please save my baby. I'm eight months pregnant. Please save my baby." Tears sprayed from my eyes as a bit of reality shed some light on this seemingly nightmarish mystery.

As I cried, panicking, the young doctor injected my I.V. with a clear solution. Almost instantaneously, I was a victim of the surrealism of my mind; trapped momentarily within a dream world. I was unable to distinguish reality from futility.

Was I dreaming? The ambulance ride, the memory of the angry woman, the pregnancy, and my mother finally expressing her emotions; was it real? Was this all in my head? I didn't feel and inch of pain. How could I have forgotten about my baby? It felt like a nightmare, but was it?

ALSO FROM NICOLE

"This book will make it hard for you to sleep."-Shaunta Kenerly

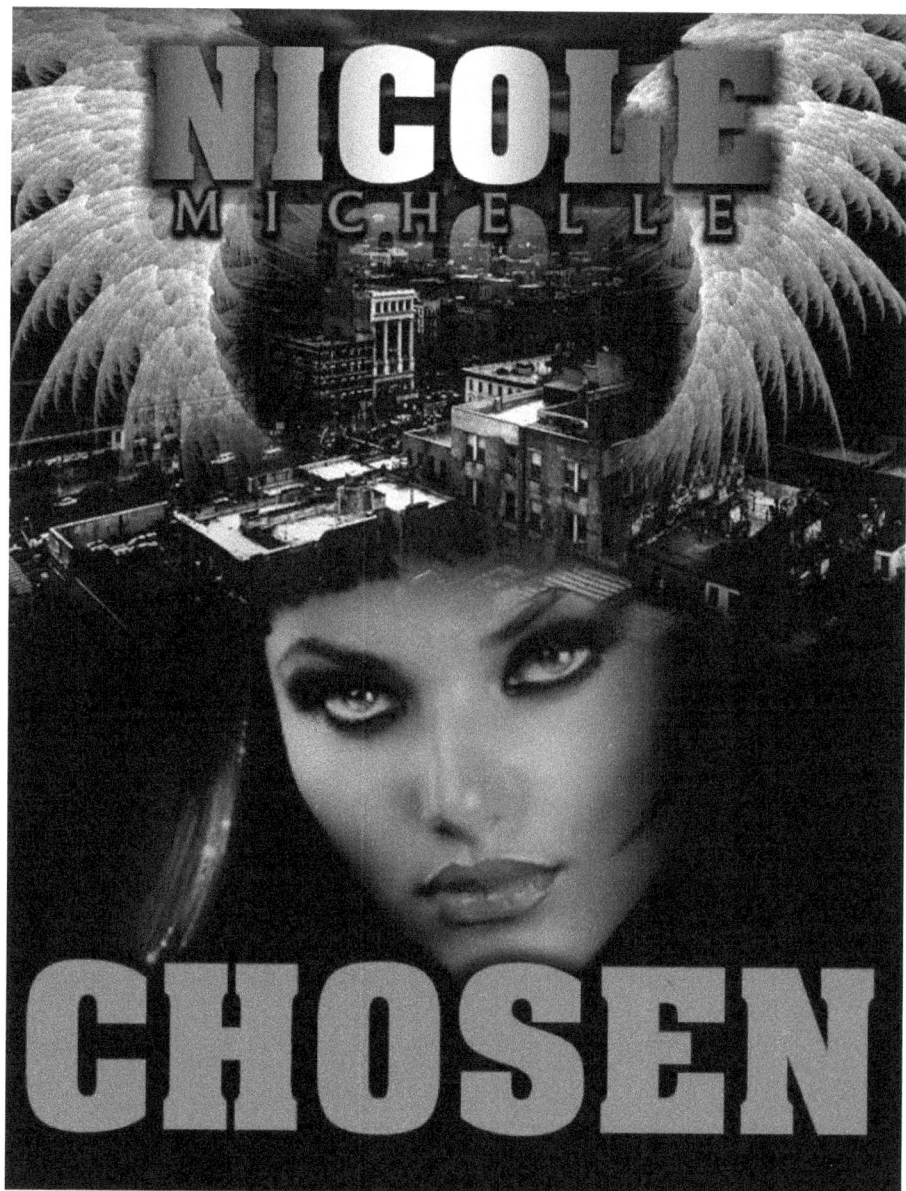

THANK YOU FOR YOUR PURCHASE. PLEASE BE SURE TO CHECK OUT THE REST OF OUR SELECTION.

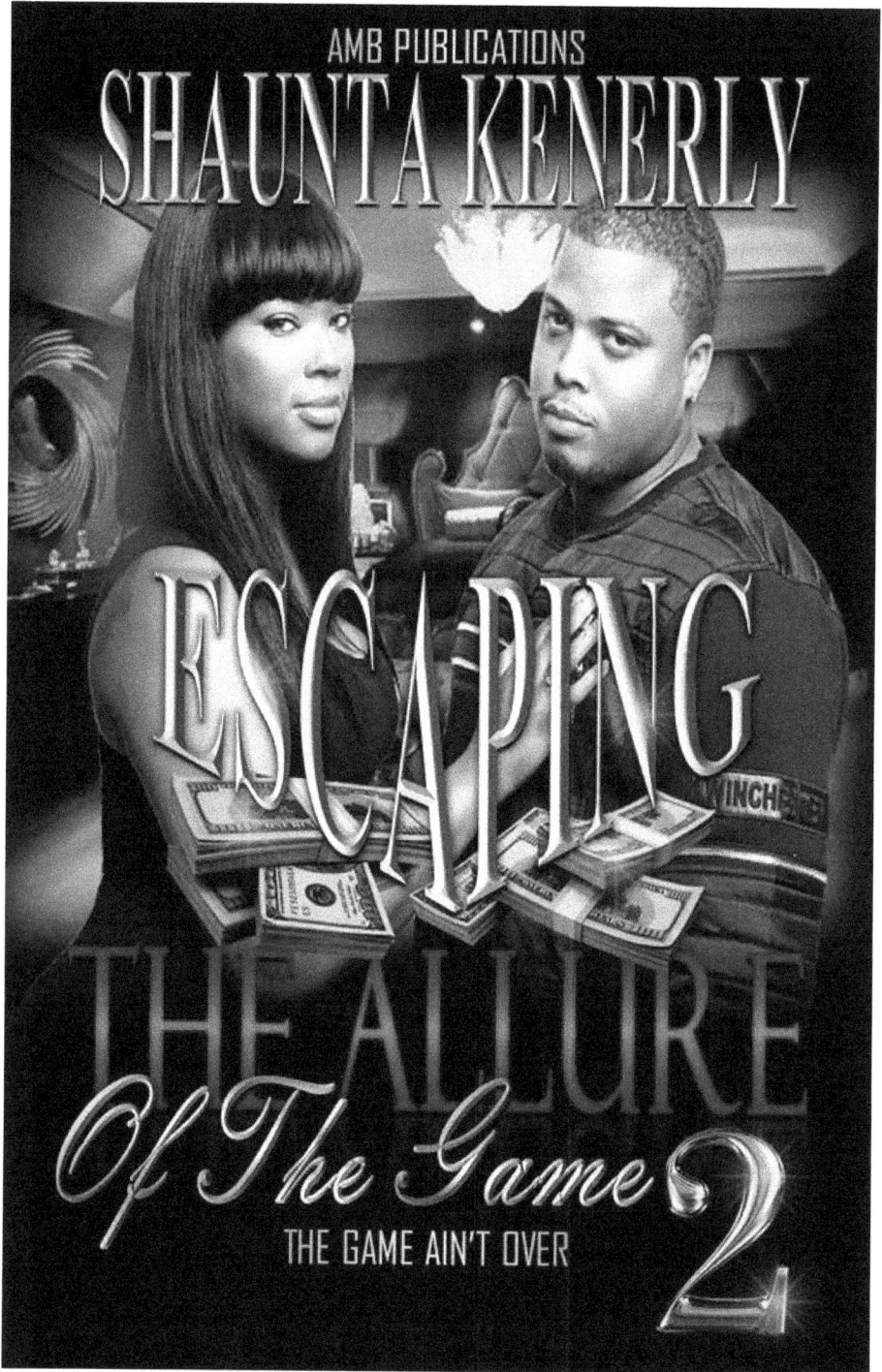

URBAN AND STREET LIT. NOVELS
amb Kenerly PRESENTS
PUBLICATIONS
AVAILABLE NOW
Dannaye Carter
Boutique
MISS KIM
MICHAEL NIXON
Don't Knock It Till You Try It
Between The Sheets
"PILLOW TALK"
HEART of A THUG
NICOLE
CHOSEN
From Pyramids To Projects
KEITH SPOKEN VOCALLY MOORE
THE PROVERBS
TREASURE
SHAUNTA KENERLY
A NOVEL BY
Jasmine Cotton
Hear Me Out
ESCAPING THE ALLURE OF THE GAME
BIRD FLU THE SERIES
SHAUNTA KENERLY
BIRD FLU THE SERIES
SHAUNTA KENERLY
I DON'T TRUST YOU
nook
BAM! BOOKS-A-MILLION
amazon kindle

www.ingramcontent.com/pod-product-compliance
Lightning Source LLC
Chambersburg PA
CBHW061721020426
42331CB00006B/1039